SPRITE AND MIDGET

PAST AND PRESENT

TERRY HORLER

AMBERLEY

Acknowledgements

I take this opportunity to thank the following for all their help and assistance in producing this book.

David Polonowski, www.david.polonowski.com, who captured all of the images for this book unless otherwise stated. Additional photographs come from Richard Gunn, John Davies, and Andy Cross.

Thank you to the Midget & Sprite Club, www.midgetandspriteclub.co.uk, and its members, who supplied all of the cars and helped with the contents.

Finally, to Amberley Publishing, www.amberley-books.com, for publishing this work.

Terry Horler
Yate 2016

First published 2016

Amberley Publishing
The Hill, Stroud,
Gloucestershire, GL5 4EP

www.amberley-books.com

ISBN: 978 1 4456 5553 6 (print)
ISBN: 978 1 4456 5554 3 (ebook)

British Library Cataloguing in Publication Data.
A catalogue record for this book is available from the British Library.

Typeset in 10pt on 13pt Celeste.
Typesetting by Amberley Publishing.
Printed in the UK.

The subject of Sprites and Midgets can cover a wide field, as these examples attempt to demonstrate.

Contents

About this Book

The Austin-Healey Sprite and MG Midget have enjoyed enormous popularity over the years; the number of books and magazine articles dedicated to these wonderful little cars lay testament to this. But, has every last word been written on the subject or does the story continue? The fact that you have this book in your hands proves that interest does indeed continue. The aim of this book is bring the story into the present day, and to help answer the questions that owners and potential owners face in today's world.

To give sufficient room for this, I have deliberately avoided a couple of areas that have been so well covered elsewhere: firstly, the huge and highly successful motor-sport career that these cars have enjoyed; also, the numerous attempts to re-style the original product by way of utilising partly, or completely different, body panels. Available from a wide variety of after-market manufacturers throughout the years, all the offerings with which an owner could re-style their Sprite or Midget could easily fill yet another book. So I will stick to the more general field of interest in these cars today by looking at the very familiar face of the Sprite and Midget that we can all recognise.

Produced from 1958 to 1979, these cars refused to simply fade away in the ensuing years. Certainly, there were some very quiet and gloomy periods – times when they were almost forgotten, values were rock bottom, and the thought of spending any serious money or time on these cars was but for the few. Then came the realisation that the small sports car had almost vanished from our roads. The makers of the Triumph Spitfire and Honda S800 also believed that forthcoming safety and emission regulations, particularly in the lucrative North American market, would soon preclude any new small, soft-top cars from being viable. Instead, manufacturers concentrated on the sports coupe market. Other than Reliant, who bucked the trend by introducing their Scimitar SS1 in 1984, anyone who wanted a small, inexpensive sports car would have to search for something older, and hopefully still useable. Perhaps this gap in the new car market was primarily responsible for enthusiasts beginning to restore the older, ageing, rusting, bent and battered Sprites and Midgets. But then, there was another factor to consider – the fun factor!

Without doubt, Sprites and Midgets, or 'Spridgets', to save on the word count, are just about the best fun for the money in terms of sports cars of all time. They were when they were new; they were in the forgotten years; and yes, they still are today. This is really the theme of this book, looking at how an inexpensive little sports car, designed in the middle of the last century, has survived into a world that its creators would never have imagined. Cars that the industry abandoned are still sought after, used and enjoyed by a new generation of enthusiasts, as well as quite a few original enthusiasts too!

The following chapters follow from where the story began to where we are now. What is it like to purchase and own one of these cars today? I could just simply sum this up by saying, 'It's a lot of fun'. Please read on for a more comprehensive explanation.

Designed in a time before motorways and speed bumps, the compact dimensions made Spridgets ideal for country lanes and getting places where larger vehicles struggle. With soft top stowed, all-round visibility allows occupants to enjoy an unspoilt view of wherever they go.

Introduction

The Austin-Healey Sprite and MG Midget were the result of a very timely agreement between just two men: Leonard Lord, the managing director of the British Motor Corporation (BMC), and Donald Healey, founder of the Donald Healey Motor Co. Ltd (DHMC). These men were no strangers: in 1952, the DHMC had designed and built a new sports car, the Healey 100, the prototype appearing on the Healey stand at the 1952 Earls Court Motor Show. The Healey 100 used major components from BMC, including engine, gearbox and axles. As a small company, the DHMC could never hope to manufacture this car in any large numbers from their small factory in Warwick. Leonard Lord inspected the new Healey at the show and offered a solution. BMC would undertake the manufacture of the Healey 100 and retain the DHMC as consultants for the development of what would now become the Austin-Healey 100. The DHMC would receive royalties from BMC upon sales. The agreement and the car proved successful. Although BMC were the largest mass producer of sports cars, by the mid-1950s BMC had found that they had strayed away from the small-engine-capacity sports-car market. At a meeting between Lord and Healey in 1956, the men agreed to work on a new sports car to fill this once-popular area. Again, the new car would use as many BMC components as possible, but in an all-new body unit. Unlike any previous mass-produced sports cars, the new one would have no separate chassis unit. Instead, the body would be of unitary, or monocoque, construction. This would ensure that both production costs and weight could be kept to a minimum. Enter the Austin-Healey Sprite on 20 May 1958. Production commenced in March 1958, ahead of launch date, at the MG factory at Abingdon, MG being a part of the BMC group of companies. But, meanwhile, where is the MG Midget?

The MG Midget would not appear until June 1961, one month after the original Sprite was replaced by a Mk II version. Hence, in terms of the Mk nomenclature, the Midget would always be behind the equivalent Sprite by one. However, it would not be behind in specification; the Midget was a sort of deluxe option compared to the Sprite, carrying a slightly higher price tag for the privilege. The unofficial but popular term of 'Spridget' was coined as a collective name for the twosome, especially useful in later years when it became increasingly difficult to spot the difference between the two.

The following chapters will describe the evolution of the Spridget during the twenty-one years of production and the 354,164 examples built during that time. Some 75 per cent of total production was exported, mostly to North America where both Austin-Healey and MG were very respected marques. Production ceased in December 1979 prior to the closure of the MG factory at Abingdon in 1981. However, this is not the end of the story for this book; we continue into the present day for these cars.

Why should a small, inexpensive, mass-produced sports car be so popular over half a century on? Designed at a time when the average life of a vehicle was around twelve years, how have these survived to continue to provide enjoyment for their present-day owners? What is it like to purchase, own and maintain a Spridget in a time long after their expected life span? Who better to ask than those who own Spridgets today, and now proudly display them in this book?

Although the sun set on production in December 1979, it has since dawned to see many examples still being enjoyed well into the next century. What nicer way to finish a day than with an evening drive in a Spridget?

1

Identification

With a twenty-one-year production period, many changes were made in order to improve the basic product for the customer, also to meet the current safety, construction and emission regulations. Some changes were of a very minor nature, while others were sufficiently significant to prompt a change in the Mark (Mk) nomenclature. Sprites and Midgets are defined by an advance in the Mk number. Officially, neither Sprite nor Midget advanced beyond Mk IV for the Sprite or Mk III for the Midget. However, defining a version by just the Mk number can be rather misleading. At times, BMC seemed to have forgotten to use this system when significant changes were made. Fortunately, there is another, and far more definitive, way to recognise each version, using the Vehicle Identification Number (VIN) prefix. This is stamped onto an aluminium plate mounted on the frame rail, just behind the left-hand front damper unit. The plate states 'CAR NUMBER' but, in modern parlance, it is the VIN plate. It is the prefix to the actual VIN that identifies the version far more accurately than the Mk number does. The positioning and number of the VIN stampings varied for export market versions in later years.

The number on this plate should agree with the VIN on the vehicle registration document, or the V5C as is current in the UK. Documentation errors are not unknown, with mistakes sometimes having been made when handwritten registration documents were subsequently transferred to later registration records. The engine number was never recorded on the car number plate, despite a space being provided for this. There is another

The VIN plate containing the Car Number is mounted just behind the left-hand front damper unit. The engine number was not stamped on this, despite there being a place for it.

No mistaking why the nicknames 'Frogeye' or 'Bugeye' clearly describe the Sprite Mk I. The bonnet-mounted headlamps were originally intended to retract, but the idea was dropped at prototype stage.

identification plate between the door hinges in the door pillar. This is the body number plate used for production purposes; it is not an identification number used for registration purposes. The factory used this number prior to the VIN plate being issued to each vehicle on the production line. The body number plate is located in the right-hand door pillar for the Sprite Mk I and in the left-hand door pillar for all subsequent versions.

The easiest version to recognise is the Sprite Mk I, which had a very different appearance to the later versions. Fondly known as the 'Frogeye' in the UK or 'Bugeye' in North America or Australia, the headlamps mounted in the top of the bonnet explain the nickname perfectly. At the other end of production, the Midget 1500 became known as the 'Rubber Bumpered' Midget for very obvious reasons again – even though the large, energy-absorbing bumpers were not made of rubber! Only one other version gained a common nickname: the 'Round Arch' Midget (1972–1974). The rear wheel arches were reshaped to expose the complete circumference of the tyre and were produced with a small flair – the front wheel arches did not receive a matching flair. A reversion to 'Square Arch' followed for the Midget 1500 to increase strength in the rear of the body. Other than these three versions, all the others are commonly referred to as Spridgets by most observers; the following explains how to identify each version by the VIN prefix. However, it should be noted that additions to the basic prefix were used to further describe export variations and to identify the model year. From here on, you will know exactly how to identify each of the versions.

A typical Spridget of the middle era. From October 1969, the difference between Sprite and Midget was confined to the badging. Aftermarket alloy wheels and a fibreglass hardtop adorn this example.

When announced on the home market in January 1972, the 'Round Arch' Midget had no Sprite equivalent. The Sprite finished in July 1971.

The Midget 1500 soon became known as the 'Rubber-bumpered Midget' for rather obvious reasons, even though the bumpers were not made of rubber. A return to 'square' rear wheel arches seemed an odd move but disguised the increase in ride height of the suspension, in addition to putting some strength back into the rear end.

Sprites and Midgets, as defined by the VIN prefix

The Sprites		The Midgets	
Sprite Mk I 948cc Frogeye May 1959–May 1961	AN5	No equivalent Midget	
Sprite Mk II 948cc Drum front brakes May 1961–Oct 1962	HAN6	Midget Mk I 948cc Drum front brakes June 1961–Oct 1962	GAN1
Sprite Mk II 1098cc Disc front brakes Oct. 1962–March 1964	HAN7	Midget Mk I 1098cc Disc front brakes Oct. 1962–March 1964	GAN2
Sprite Mk III 1098cc Winding windows March 1964–Oct. 1966	HAN8	Midget Mk II 1098cc Winding windows March 1964–Oct. 1966	GAN3

Sprite	Prefix	Midget	Prefix
Sprite Mk IV 1275cc Folding soft top Oct. 1966–Oct. 1969	HAN9	Midget Mk III 1275cc Folding soft top Oct. 1966–Oct. 1969	GAN4
Sprite Mk IV 1275cc Facelift Oct. 1969–Dec 1970	HAN10	Midget Mk III 1275cc Facelift Oct. 1969–1972	GAN5
Austin Sprite Healey name discontinued Jan. 1971–July 1971	AAN10	As above	
		Midget Mk III 1275cc Round Arch Oct. 1971–Nov. 1974	GAN5
		Midget 1500 1493cc Rubber bumpered Nov. 1974–Dec. 1979	GAN6

The VIN prefix could be followed by further identification letters prior to the actual number. These are as follows:

L	Left-hand drive
U	North American versions from 1967
U	followed by A to M, these are the model-year identifiers from 1970 to 1979
YH	An Australian-assembled Sprite prefix.
YGN	An Australian-assembled Midget from November 1967 prefix.

The allocation of the actual vehicle identification numbers is given in the following chapters. Simply subtracting the first from last number for each does not necessarily equate to the actual number built. Some numbers were not used or assembled as complete vehicles.

The VIN suffix

From the beginning of 1967, BMC applied a suffix to the VIN; this suffix letter identified the UK assembly plant. For Abingdon, this was a 'G'. This is often incorrectly shown as a '6' on the registration document. For a short while in early 1967, 489 Sprites and 476 Midgets were completed at Cowley and carried the suffix 'M'.

The aluminium engine number plate is often missing from the A-series engine following reconditioning. Without this, identifying the original application of the engine is difficult.

Identification by engine number

The engine number was never stamped into the VIN plate; instead, there were the words, 'See engine'. So we now look at the engine. From 1958 to 1974, the engine was a BMC 'A' Series unit of 948cc, 1098cc and finally 1275cc capacities. These engines had a small, oblong aluminium plate riveted to the top face of the cylinder block, just above the dynamo or alternator. Spridgets carried an engine number prefix that was particular to each version and not shared by any other model in the BMC range of vehicles. Having the original engine can be a big plus point when originality is important to an owner. Often, the riveted plate is removed when an engine is fully reconditioned, and not replaced. The original capacity of the engine can still be established, however. By looking at the front left-hand face of the cylinder block, near to the fuel pump mounting boss, the capacity is either revealed on a metal plate or by casting numerals. Engines were produced in either high- or low-compression ratio type, the latter to suit certain overseas markets. The last letter of the prefix being either an 'H' for high or 'L' for low compression ratio. The following table assumes the more common 'H' application.

Should a factory-reconditioned engine be fitted, a new number plate is applied with a new identifying prefix.

VIN Prefix	Original Engine Number Prefix Home market	Factory Recondition Prefix
AN5	9C-U-H	8G10
HAN6 & GAN1	9CG-U-H (very early examples only)	
HAN6 & GAN1	9CG-DA-H	8G16 (H) or 8G17 (L)
HAN7 & GAN2	10CG-DA-H	8G124 (H) or 8G125 (L)
HAN8 & GAN3	10CC-DA-H	8G150 (H) or 8G149 (L)
HAN9 & GAN4	12CC-DA-H	8G180 (H) or 8G179 (L)
HAN9 & GAN4	12CE-DA-H	
HAN10 & GAN5	12CE-DA-H	
AAN10	12CE-DA-H	

GAN5	12CE-DA-H	
GAN5 Round Arch	12V586FH	
GAN5	12V588FH	
GAN5	12V778FH	All as above

1275cc engines for the North American market carried varying stages of emission control equipment; these engines carried the following prefix markings.

HAN9 & GAN4	12CD-DA-H	8G189 (H) or 8G190 (L)
GAN5	12CJ-DA-H	As above
GAN5 (Round arch)	12V587ZL	38G506 (L only)
GAN5 (Round arch)	12V671ZL	As above

From 1974, the Triumph 1493cc engine for the Midget 1500 (GAN6) can be identified as follows. The number is stamped into a projection on the rear left-hand side of the cylinder block.

Prefix	Suffix	Application
FP	E	Home market
FP	UE	North America
FP	UCE	California

Body number prefix

A body number was applied prior to the VIN plate being allocated during final assembly. The body number and VIN were not in numerical sequence.

Version	Body Number Plate Location	Prefix
Sprite Mk I	Right-hand door pillar between the door hinges	BAE
Sprite Mk II	Left-hand door pillar between the door hinges	ABL

The body number appears on a painted plate between the door hinges. This number was only used for production purposes and should not appear on the vehicle registration document in place of the VIN.

This continued until the end of production of the Sprite.

Midget	Left-hand door pillar between the hinges	GBE
Midget 1500	On the bonnet slam panel (home market)	GB47T
Midget 1500	As above (North America market)	GU47T

Other markings

In addition to the above, certain other markings were included during production. John Thompson Motor Pressings stamped a number into the upper footwell panel, near to the aperture for the pedal box assembly. This number was not recorded in the factory records but approximates to the Car Number. This was discontinued in the very early 1960s.

With the introduction of the 1275cc versions, the Car Number was stamped into the floor just ahead of the jacking point cross member, on the right-hand side for UK versions. For North American versions, the Car Number was stamped into the right-hand front damper mounting platform.

The bonnet badge for the Sprite Mk I declared it was an Austin-Healey and included the Austin shield.

Simply badged as a Sprite from the rear. Austin-Healey did not appear on the rear badge until October 1969. Only the Sprite MK I used this golden-arrow design.

The Sprite Mk II bonnet badge now spread some wings; this remained for all Sprites until October 1969.

The Sprite Mk II boot badge, which served until October 1969. Again, Austin-Healey only appeared on the bonnet badge. The Frogeye bumperettes were an option on the very early Sprite Mk II. The L type boot handle was soon replaced with a T type handle.

The Midget grille badge, which served from introduction to the October 1969 facelift.

The MG Midget boot badge was quite an elaborate item; this also served from introduction to the October 1969 facelift.

From the October 1969 facelift, this was a common grille for both Sprite and Midget with a central badge to identify which was which. Here, the owner has a few other badges to display as well.

From October 1969, the facelift Sprite boot badge now revealed the manufacturer to be Austin-Healey or, from January 1971, simply Austin. This latter badge is now unobtainable and a prized item for Austin Sprite owners.

Just as the Sprite boot badge displayed the full make and model information from October 1969, the MG Midget was now reduced to just the famous MG octagon logo but without the model name. This served until the end of production in 1979.

The Midget 1500 grille badge, or perhaps, 'air intake' badge. The actual grille was behind the rubber bumper.

2

Into Production

With the agreement made between Leonard Lord and Donald Healey to embark on a new small Austin-Healey, the DHMC at Warwick set to work to build two prototypes. Donald Healey's son, Geoff, led the project, while Gerry Coker, who styled the Healey 100, was awarded the task of styling the new car. Barry Bilbie, Healey's engineer, produced the chassis-work design. Les Ireland was later brought in when Gerry Coker accepted a new job in the USA. Most of the mechanical components were drawn from existing BMC production vehicles, notably the Austin A35 and Morris Minor, with some components being modified to suit the new application. Overall, cost was kept to a minimum in order to offer the new car at an affordable price to a younger customer and yet still generate a profit, a portion of which would be paid to the DHMC.

The prototypes were codenamed Q1 and Q2 by the DHMC but more affectionately known as 'Tiddler' by those involved with the project. With the prototypes completed and tested, the project was then handed over to BMC for production engineering to develop into a saleable product. BMC applied the code name ADO 13 (Amalgamated Drawing Office). Certain changes were made, but not all with the approval of the DHMC design team. In an attempt to keep costs down and to simplify production, the gauge thickness of the steel in certain highly stressed areas of the body unit were reduced. This was to cause a major weakness problem in the early days of production. To correct this, early body units had to have strengthening brackets and gussets welded into the rear quarters before more substantial strengthening in this, and the engine compartment, could go into production. However, other than this and some early revisions to the cooling system, the new car enjoyed a fairly trouble-free launch.

The name 'Sprite' was chosen and announced on 20 May 1958. Actual production had begun in March of that year in order to build up a stock for the dealerships. To produce the Sprite, BMC would again take the responsibility with the DHMC to receive royalties on sales and to develop the Sprite through a motor-sport programme and further research. BMC was a vast organisation with many factories acquired from the various mergers and takeovers of constituent companies. BMC chose the MG factory at Abingdon to assemble the Sprite, with component parts supplied by other factories in the BMC group. The numerous industry supply companies, such as Lucas for the electrics, Lockheed for brakes and hydraulic systems, and Smiths for the instruments and heaters, would also contribute as many 'off the shelf' components as possible so as to minimise production costs.

Initially, the major floor and frame structure was produced by John Thompson Motor Pressings of Wolverhampton. These were sent to Pressed Steel at Swindon for the body panels to be attached. At this stage, a body number would be applied before the complete body unit was sent to the Cowley factory for painting. Now gleaming, the body units arrived at the MG factory at Abingdon for full assembly, utilising all the many other delivered components. At Abingdon, the body number would be handwritten, in yellow crayon, on the inside of the bonnet and the rear axle tunnel. The bonnet would then be removed to ease the assembly process, being reunited with the matching body number nearing the end of the production line, thus ensuring both paint match and fit.

Although a body number had been allocated and applied prior to assembly, MG had a tradition of assembling cars with separate body and chassis units. Here, tradition was maintained by allocating the Sprite a chassis number in addition to the body number, even though body and chassis were all one unit. The chassis number appeared as 'Car Number' on the attached plate; in today's parlance, this is the Vehicle Identification Number (VIN). The VIN plate could only be fitted once assembly was under way and it was known whether the Sprite would be a right- or left-hand drive version, the VIN prefix containing an 'L' if assembled to left-hand drive specification. Prior to 1968, the bare body unit was fully ambidextrous; it could be assembled as either right- or left-hand drive. The dashboard would be identified against the VIN in handwritten crayon on the reverse, determining whether it was left- or right-hand drive, its trim colour, and if there were any apertures for option extras such as the heater control or windscreen washer. This would ensure that the correct dashboard would be fitted to the correct Car Number on the line.

Although the MG factory was the main assembly facility, some overseas markets took on final assembly from a kit of parts known as CKD units (Completely Knocked Down). These were sent by BMC to their overseas assembly plants, the largest being the BMC Zetland plant in Australia. Australian regulations made the import of completed new vehicles expensive. However, any manufacturer producing within Australia could take advantage of avoiding these regulations and high import tax penalties. Australian-assembled versions can be identified by a 'Y' appearing in the VIN prefix. By using locally sourced parts or resources, overseas manufacturers enjoyed a considerable advantage over those importing complete vehicles. At the beginning of 1967, a number of Sprites and Midgets were completed at the Cowley factory. This may have been done to clear a hold-up in production shortly after the 1275cc engine had been announced. The first 900 or so Spridgets assembled with the new engine were held back, as these engines had a lubrication and crankshaft problem.

In 1968, BMC was merged into the British Leyland group (B-L). This now included Standard Triumph, the manufacturer of the Spridget's head-on rival, the Triumph Spitfire. The first effect of this appeared on a facelift for the Sprite Mk IV and Midget Mk III from October 1969. Other than badging, all the previous detail differences were removed. A small B-L badge was added to the front wing panel.

At the end of 1970, B-L severed links with the DHMC and the name of Austin-Healey disappeared. Initially, Sprite production continued from January 1971 but no longer with the Healey name included, to be badged simply as an Austin Sprite. This continued until July 1971, when the final Sprite was made. However, the name Sprite did reappear on a version of the Mini for a short while. The merger provided a more sizeable impact in 1974, when the 1493cc engine from the Spitfire was then shared by the new Midget 1500.

Arguably, this did allow the Midget to continue in the North American market for another five years. Without this option, the Midget might have succumbed in 1974 and left just the Spitfire as B-L's small sports car.

When the MG Midget was announced in 1961 (ADO 47), production would be on the same assembly line as the Sprite; this would continue until its discontinuation in July 1971. The Midget continued until 7 December 1979, when the very last one came off the production line. This car was retained by the manufacturer and is currently on display at the Heritage Motor Centre at Gaydon, Warwickshire.

The very last Midget 1500 was made on 7 December 1979, the MG factory at Abingdon closing in 1981. The MGB was the last model to remain in production there. Like this example, the very last Midget was finished in black and is retained in the manufacturer's collection at the Motor Centre, Gaydon, Warwickshire.

3

The Sprite Mk I

As announced, the new Sprite was not referred to as the Mk I; this nomenclature was coined when the Mk II came along in May 1961. However, the nicknames of 'Frogeye' or 'Bugeye' was very soon applied for very obvious reasons. Although many existing BMC components were under the skin, this was a very new car in every other sense. It filled a gap in the small sports car market, which had existed for many years; it was aimed at a younger customer base, who would hopefully become loyal and future customers of BMC products. It not only had a completely fresh look but, at a very modest list price, it was sure to attract a lot of fresh new interest.

The front bumper with over-riders was an optional extra for the home market. Without a bumper, a steel plinth, retained by four screws to the front valance, mounted the number plate beneath the chromed grille. More often, a stick-on number plate between the headlamps provided a cheaper and more sporting appearance.

Model identification

VIN allocation – AN5/501 to AN5/50116
The last complete Sprite Mk I assembled at Abingdon was AN5/49584 in November 1960.
Further production was for CKD assembly overseas.
Number built – 48,987

The Body Unit

Monocoque, or unitary constructed body shells, were not new in terms of saloon cars. However, this type of construction had never been used for a mass-produced sports car. For the saloon car, the roof and vertical posts are a part of the stressed structure to provide overall rigidity. As an open car, the Sprite would have to be sufficiently rigid in the floor pan alone to keep the front and rear ends together. Hence, deep box-section sills spanned the small door openings. The sills did not contain an inner stiffener or membrane panel; instead, the gauge thickness of the inner and outer sill pressings had to be sufficient to give the necessary beam strength. The single-skin floor was pressed with transverse stiffening ribs, with longitudinal stiffeners being welded to the floor for further strength and load transfer. The transmission tunnel was a large box section enclosing the propeller shaft, the front end being left open under the gearbox. This added further stiffness to the floor. A transverse box section in front of the seats contained the jacking points at the outer ends and gearbox mounting in the centre. The rear axle tunnel and heel panel provided the mounting points for the rear quarter-elliptic road springs. Again, this was a novel idea that deleted the need for any spring location points behind the rear axle. However, this placed the entire rear axle loading in the rear edge of the floor pan. A strong, thick gauge box located each spring within the rear bulkhead and floor area.

This clever use of box sections provided a very good strength-to-weight ratio throughout the construction. Whether to keep costs down or to provide more rear-end strength, no boot lid was provided in the rear shroud panel. This was a feature which did not prove very popular with owners, with a dive into the darkness and depths of the boot. This was

Short doors were required to maximise the beam strength across the door gaps. Reduced knee flexibility can sometimes bring about a reluctant end to ownership. The lack of exterior door handles produces a clean line but may puzzle first-time passengers.

The one-piece steel bonnet is heavy to lift and required a knack to open and close safely. Minor damage could make this knack even more of a challenge. Aftermarket fibreglass bonnets, either to the original style or modified, became a popular swap.

not the only design flaw in terms of user friendliness. The rear hinged bonnet included the front wings and front grille panel and valence. Owners found this heavy and awkward to open and close, especially if the optional (home-market) front bumper was fitted, which obscured the handle. Furthermore, even minor accident damage could knock the whole thing out of alignment. Hence many original steel bonnets were replaced with aftermarket fibreglass bonnets of original or of a re-styled appearance.

Engine

The BMC A-Series engine had been in production since 1952, firstly as an 803cc for the Austin A30 and then from 1956 as a 948cc for the Austin A35 and Morris Minor saloon cars. This was a conventional four-cylinder, overhead valve unit of cast-iron construction. The five-port cylinder head was arranged with two siamesed inlet ports with central Siamese exhaust port for the middle two cylinders. Individual exhaust ports served front and rear cylinders. The steel crankshaft was carried in three main bearings. The camshaft was driven by a single row chain. For the Sprite, some improved internal components were employed to better withstand the expected antics of a different type of owner! Power was a claimed 42.5 bhp with an 8.3:1 compression ratio. A full-flow oil filter was fitted to an extension piece to the alloy mounting used for the A35. This was required to allow clearance to the right-hand frame rail beneath.

With just 42.5 bhp to provide the fun, the twin-carburettor version of the Austin A35 engine proved reliable and economical. Tuning potential was very good, with a wide variety of modifications being available – even a Shorrock supercharger kit.

Fuel & Exhaust Systems

A pressed-steel, 6-gallon fuel tank was mounted beneath the boot floor. An AC mechanical fuel pump was fitted to the left-hand side of the cylinder block. This fed twin 1.125-inch SU H1 carburettors mounted on an alloy inlet manifold. A Cooper wire mesh air filter was provided for each carburettor. A steel heat shield was fitted between the carburettors and inlet manifold to provide some insulation from the cast-iron exhaust manifold beneath. The exhaust manifold was carried over from the Austin A35 but with the hot spot connection to the inlet manifold blanked off. The steel exhaust pipe was finished off with a single, straight-through type silencer mounted beside the fuel tank. It sounded just like a sports car should!

Gearbox & Clutch

This also came from the same source as the engine but was fitted with a shorter, chrome-plated gear lever. The enclosed transmission tunnel and frame rails precluded the gearbox from being removed from beneath. Instead, the engine could be removed either in unit with or before gearbox removal. The Borg & Beck nine-spring clutch of 6.25-inch diameter was operated hydraulically via a carbon-graphite release bearing.

Front Suspension & Steering

Again, the Austin A35 provided an instant source of lower wishbone, kingpin, stub axle and damper arrangement. The Armstrong lever arm damper also doubled as the upper suspension link and bearing. However, the A35 used a steering box and drag link arrangement for the steering. The Morris Minor used a much better rack and pinion unit, so this was used along with revised steering arms to the stub axles. This provided a good steering and independent front suspension system, but it was one that was also prone to wear if not maintained properly.

Rear Axle & Suspension

A modified A35 axle was used along with a 4.22:1 crown wheel and pinion unit. The axle locations were revised to enable the fourteen-leaf quarter-elliptic springs to attach from below the axle and the radius arms from above the axle. Although the axle was firmly located longitudinally, only the quarter-elliptic springs offered any transverse location. The use of this type of spring and the associated heavy loadings imposed, even on such a lightweight, caused problems. Spring settlement and breakage of spring leaves was a common complaint. BMC soon offered a 'heavy duty' eleven-leaf spring using thicker leaves. Armstrong lever arm dampers controlled the suspension.

Brakes

The 7-inch-diameter drum brakes were supplied by Lockheed, twin leading shoe at the front and single leading shoe at the rear. A tandem master cylinder, which also served the hydraulic clutch, was mounted in a pedal box above the driver's feet. A chromed handbrake lever operated on the rear drum brakes via a cable and reaction rods mounted on the rear axle.

Wheels & Tyres

Pressed steel wheels, 13 inches by 3.5 inches, were supplied by Rubery Owen. These were secured by four studs of 3/8 UNF threads. The wheels were pierced with twelve ventilation holes, plus two further holes within the hub cap area for brake adjustment access. Wheels were finished in aluminium paint and finished with a chromed hub cap with the letters AH pressed in. The standard tyre was a 5.20 inches by 13 inches crossply. No wire wheel option was offered by the factory. Instead, the DHMC offered wire wheels along with a disc front brake and larger rear drum brake conversion. This utilised separated brake and clutch master cylinders, mounted in a widened pedal box. These conversions were very expensive and are rare to find today. Most Mk I versions seen today with wire wheels either use the

Pierced steel disc wheels, painted in silver aluminium, were finished with a chromed hub cap with the letters 'AH' embossed in the centre. The factory did not offer a wire-wheel option for the Mk I. However, wire wheels could be ordered from the DHMC along with disc front brakes and larger diameter rear brakes.

items that were offered by the factory from 1962 onwards, or later aftermarket conversions. It should be noted that factory-fitted wire wheels from 1962 onwards utilised a slightly narrowed rear-axle casing. To fit these wire wheels to a steel disc wheel rear axle, the wire wheel half shafts do not fully engage with the differential unit.

Electrics

These were supplied by Lucas and to the industry standard of the day. A dynamo provided for a positive earth system via a voltage regulator mounted on the right-hand inner front wing. Two fuses provided protection for what was a very simple circuit, the fuse box being mounted adjacent to the regulator box. Windscreen wipers were single speed, but with self-parking blades. There was a single-speed heater fan, if the optional heater was fitted, non-self-cancelling turn indicators, the usual lighting requirements, but no headlamp flash and, of course, the horn. The main problem for the electrics seemed to be hapless owners adding their own additions to the circuitry, often very badly!

Interior & Instruments

Originally, ribbed rubber matting covered the floor areas, with ICI vynide for the covered surfaces and seats. Only the driver's seat was provided with reach adjustment. Although sparsely trimmed, the dashboard was well stocked with Smiths instruments. The rev counter was an optional extra but very few owners failed to specify this. The rev counter was cable via a small reduction gearbox mounted on the rear of the dynamo. The speedometer contained total- and trip-distance recorders. A combined gauge for engine water temperature and oil pressure was completed by a fuel-tank-contents gauge. The passenger could take advantage of a chrome-plated grab handle, mounted to the dashboard, if things started to get exciting.

Hollow doors provided plenty of elbow room and a sizeable stowage pocket. The side screens were retained by two knurled screws to the aluminium extrusion along the top of the door. Note the simple door-release lever; locking was not provided.

Passenger safety was well catered for with this chrome grab handle – or perhaps this was just a token gesture? The steel dashboard panel included a perforated section under the vinyl covering that could be easily cut out to fit the optional radio.

The flat dashboard was well stocked with Smiths instruments. The large, plastic-rimmed steering wheel was a favourite item to replace with a smaller wood- or leather-rimmed version. An original steering wheel is now something of a rarity.

Exterior

The exterior was almost devoid of any unnecessary trim, and even the chromed front bumper was an optional extra for the home market. At the rear, a pair of chromed, vertical over-riders, or bumperettes, were fitted as standard. Completing the list of chrome-plated items were the radiator grille, bonnet-release handle, number-plate light cover, fuel-filler cap and wheel hub caps. A round bonnet badge proclaimed 'Austin-Healey Sprite', while for the rear, a gold-painted arrow with the script 'Sprite' was the only external identifier.

The front bumper, when fitted, provided a neat tripping hazard, while the steel bonnet above was a 'hard-hat area' for those new to maintaining a Mk I. The learning curve could be quick and painful.

The chromed bumperettes were a standard fitment. All the rear lighting units were standard Lucas products found on other vehicles of the period. Just a simple 'Sprite' badge with no manufacturer name graced the rear panel.

Weather Equipment

A fabric soft top was supported by a removable, tubular hood frame. This can be folded and stowed into location boxes behind the seats. Initially, the frame was of fixed height but soon spring-loaded sections were included to keep the soft top taught at all times. Again, the early arrangement included nine 'Lift the Dot' fasteners along the top of the aluminium windscreen frame. The rain soon saw its way through this idea. A revised arrangement used a steel strip within the leading edge of the material to clip into the top of a suitably revised windscreen frame. The two outer Lift the Dot fasteners remained for transverse location of the soft top. Early Sprites came with fabric side curtains on a steel frame that attached to the doors by two thumb screws per side. With the hard-top option came aluminium-framed side screens, which included a sliding Perspex rear pane with a fixed front pane. These became an option to the fabric side curtains until March 1960, when the aluminium-framed side screen was standardised. A tonneau cover, with a central zip, could offer some protection when the soft top was stowed in the boot space.

A simple soft top and removable side screens take practice to remove and replace quickly. All have to be stowed behind the folding seats.

The optional tonneau cover featured a central zip in order that the passenger side could remain dry while the driver braved the elements.

A hard top was a popular option before improved soft tops were introduced. As well as a factory-supplied item, many aftermarket companies offered items of various appearance, including a full fast back design.

Options

To keep the list price attractively low, the basic specification did not include anything an owner would not need; indeed, it failed to include some items that most owners would need. Customers could order options from either the factory list or the general BMC dealership options list, which included a wider range of items. At this time, a high rate of new car purchase tax would also encompass any accessories ordered from the factory. Canny owners would order a basic Sprite, pay the invoice and then order their accessories from the dealership at a lower tax rate. At this time, many aftermarket companies began to offer all manner of accessories, modifications and other temptations for owners. Many of these period accessories are now a rarity and can be valuable in their own right. Both the DHMC and BMC offered a wide range of performance equipment for the Sprite. Everything from a wood-rim steering wheel to a supercharger kit became available. The following are the factory-listed optional extras.

Front bumper with over-riders (standard for export)
Laminated windscreen
Smith's heater/blower unit
Fresh air unit (basically, the heater unit without a heater matrix)
Sliding pane side screens (standard with hardtop and standard from March 1960)
Rev counter
Windscreen washers
Tonneau cover (Black or white)
Hardtop (Ivory white only)
Locking fuel cap
Six ply tyres
Whitewall tyres (USA only)

Although the fibreglass hard top provided an all-year-round protection from the elements, the increased noise encouraged most owners to remove it as soon as possible. Then there was the problem of where to store it.

Original colour options

Body colour	Seats and Trim	Soft Top and Tonneau	Hard Top
Speedwell Blue (to Jan 59)	Blue	Black	Ivory White
Iris Blue (from Jan 59)	Blue	Black or white	Ivory White
Dark Green (to Jan 59)	Green	Black	Ivory White
Leaf Green (from Jan 59)	Green	Black or White	Ivory White
Primrose Yellow (to Jan 59)	Black	Black	Ivory White
Nevada Beige (from Jan 59)	Cherry Red	Black or White	Ivory White
Old English White	Cherry Red or Black	Black or White	Ivory White
Cherry Red	Cherry Red	Black or White	Ivory White

4

The Sprite Mk II and the Midget Mk I

Despite the cheerful styling and character of the Sprite Mk I, sales figures were falling towards the end of 1960. BMC decided that the Sprite should become a more user-friendly car by offering a conventional boot lid and bonnet opening. To this end, they asked the DHMC to redesign the front end to include a more manageable bonnet. BMC then asked MG to redesign the rear of the car to include both a boot lid and an increased open space behind the seats. Somehow, BMC failed to advise the DHMC or MG what the other had been asked to do. Fortunately, communications between the DHMC and MG were rather better; hence, the completed makeover enjoyed some conformity – well, almost. This may explain why the front wheel arches were round while the rear arches were flat topped. To further broaden the appeal of what was now the Sprite Mk II (ADO 41), BMC introduced an MG Midget version (ADO 47). Essentially, this was a 'deluxe' option of the Sprite. Mechanically identical, interior and exterior trim upgrades also produced an upgrade in price for the new Midget. The Sprite Mk II was launched in May 1961, with the Midget Mk I released the following month. A spot of double thunder for the marketing department, no doubt. In truth, despite the amalgamation between Austin and Morris, it was only the Austin dealerships that had sold the Sprite Mk I, leaving the Morris dealerships without an equivalent to offer. In October 1962, upgrades for both versions were announced in

The Sprite Mk II was much more user friendly than the Mk I. A conventional bonnet and boot opening addressed much of early critics.

As well as a completely fresh appearance, the Sprite bonnet badge gained a pair of wings. The grille was now formed from aluminium.

the form of an increase in engine capacity from 948cc to 1098cc, along with an improved gearbox, disc front brakes, improved interior trim and an electric rev counter. Not that this latter item would have been a sales-clinching item. Despite this plethora of updates, both Sprite and Midget retained the Mk II and Mk I nomenclature respectively.

Model Identification

VIN allocation	Number built
Sprite Mk II (948cc) HAN6/101 to 24731	20,450
Sprite Mk II (1098cc) HAN7/24732 to 38828	11,215
Midget Mk I (948cc) GAN1/101 to 16183	16,080
Midget Mk I (1098cc) GAN2/16184 to 25787	9,601

The Midget Mk I upstaged the Sprite with a more elaborate grille, centre bonnet and side waistline trims. Under the skin, they were equals. (John Davies)

The Body Unit

The basic under structure was carried over from the Sprite Mk I. New rear wings and central shroud panel, to include a boot opening, were welded to the under structure.

The new rear shroud panel also provided for a longer cockpit area behind the seats, a divider now being incorporated to close off the boot space from the cockpit. At the front, the new radiator surround, which included the bonnet slam panel and front valance, was bolted to the frame rails. The new front wings were bolted to the radiator surround and to the footwell panel, just in front of the 'A' post. This had the added advantage of making any minor damage repairs by panel replacement very easy. The new front and rear ends gave the car a very different look to its predecessor. However, the sill pressing, door panel and door pillar remained unchanged, these being the only visible link to the earlier Sprite Mk I.

A boot lid, full-width chrome bumper and integrated rear-light units made the new Sprite and Midget appear a very different car to the Sprite Mk I. (John Davies)

The doors, sill panel and door pillars provide the only visual link to the Mk I Sprite. Under the skin, little had changed.

Side waistline trim strips and plain hub caps are identifying features of the Midget Mk I from the otherwise similar Sprite Mk II. The pierced wheels were replaced by plain disc wheels from December 1962 for both Sprite and Midget. (John Davies)

The 1098cc engine of the post-October versions provided a useful increase in power over the 948cc version. (Richard Gunn)

Engine

The engine initially remained at 948cc but with a revised camshaft, larger valves – now with double springs – and a raised compression ratio to 9:1. For certain export markets, a lower 8.3:1 compression ratio was offered. With 1.25-inch HS2 carburettors and an improved exhaust manifold, power rose to 46 bhp for the higher compression ratio. This version of the BMC A-Series engine was identified by the prefix '9CG'. In October 1962, this engine was replaced by a 1098cc unit with the prefix '10CG', and power output increased to 55 bhp.

Fuel & Exhaust System

The carburettors were larger 1.250-inch SU HS2 instruments fitted to a new alloy inlet manifold. New black-painted air-filter casings carried replaceable paper element filters.

Gearbox & Clutch

The very first examples used the Sprite Mk I gearbox; these could be recognised by the engine number prefix '9CG–U-H'. Soon, a close ratio version of this gearbox became available, which can be recognised by the engine number prefix '9CG-DA-H'. The 'DA' is the close ratio gearbox identifier. With the 1098cc engine, a revised gearbox with a ribbed casing became available. The gear ratios remained the same but the synchromesh was now of the baulk ring type. With the larger engine, the clutch was increased to a 7.250-inch diameter.

Front Suspension & Steering

This was carried forward from the Sprite Mk I. From January 1964, a front anti-roll bar was now listed as a factory-fitted option. The mounting points for this had been included in the front frame rails of the Sprite Mk I. The DHMC had offered an anti-roll bar from their own list of tuning equipment for the Mk I; this differed in detail to the latest BMC item. Both types utilised the same frame-mounting points.

A conventional boot lid provided easy access to the spare wheel and a reasonable amount of luggage space. This is somewhat reduced when the side screens, soft top and frame are stowed away. A luggage rack, as seen here, was a popular addition when touring. Some owners mounted the spare wheel to the boot lid.

Rear Axle & Suspension

Also carried forward from the Sprite Mk I. With the arrival of the 1098cc, a wire wheel option became available, which meant changes to the axle casing, half shafts and hubs. See 'Wheels & Tyres'.

Brakes

For the 948cc versions, the all-round drum system from the Mk I was retained. From May 1962, the single-piston rear slave cylinders were replaced by twin-piston cylinders mounted on revised back plates. Brake adjustment was now effected by a cone and tappet arrangement via a square-headed adjuster behind the back plate. With the introduction of the 1098cc versions, 8.250-inch-diameter disc front brakes were introduced. The tandem brake master cylinder now had 0.75-inch-diameter bores; drum-braked versions used a cylinder with 0.875-inch-diameter bores for brake and clutch.

Wheels & Tyres

For the HAN6 & GAN1, the ventilated, pressed steel wheels were carried over from the Sprite Mk I. However, the Midget Mk I would not have the pressed-in AH lettering but instead used just a plain chromed hub cap. Wire wheels were introduced as an option shortly after the introduction of the 1098cc engine. The 13-inch-by-4-inch sixty-spoke wheels were secured by double-eared spinners onto a splined hub. These had a left-hand thread on the right-hand side. A 1-inch-narrower rear axle was used to allow for the increased track of the wire wheels and hubs. The square-topped rear wheel arches allowed minimal tyre clearance. At the front, the splined hub required a revised disc brake. The ventilated steel disc wheels were replaced by plain steel disc wheels in December 1962; all wheels were finished in aluminium paint. Standard tyres were Dunlop 5.20 x 13.

The Sprite Mk II dashboard now had toggle switches and minor revisions to the warning lights within the speedo and rev counter. The Sprite retained the passenger grab handle, a feature not included in the Midget, which had an MG badge instead.

Electric

Lucas spade connectors now replaced the previous screw connectors to the various electrical components. The dashboard indicator repeater warning light was now connected to a resistor in the main light switch to reduce the glare in dark conditions. For the 1098cc version, the cable-driven rev counter was replaced by an electric rev counter.

Interior & Instruments

Toggle switches replaced the push/pull and rotating light switch of the Mk I. To demonstrate the 'deluxe' nature of the Midget Mk I, the instruments were now marked as Jaeger items; in reality, they were just remarked Smiths items. The Sprite retained the dash-mounted passenger grab handle, while the Midget received an MG badge instead. Presumably, Midget drivers were expected to be far less frightening for passengers than Sprite drivers! For the HAN7/GAN2 versions, an electric rev counter replaced the cable-driven item. All instruments now reverted to being Smiths-marked items. Improved interior trim was included for the HAN7/GAN2 versions with a padded roll above and below the dashboard. The previously painted area of the doors was now finished with trim material. Amusingly, a rear compartment seat cushion was offered as an optional extra, with additional knee room for any rear seat occupants not being possible unless the front seats were adjusted fully forward. A clever marketing ploy that at least looked attractive in the sales brochure.

The post-October 1962 interior featured an improved trim with a padded roll above and below the dashboard. Door panels were now fully trimmed. The optional rear seat cushion did not provide for much leg room. Instruments reverted to Smiths from Jaeger for the Midget MK1 (GAN2). The rev counter is now an electric item for both Sprite and Midget with the 1098cc engine. (John Davies)

Removable side screens, soft-top frame, tonneau rail and storage bag gave owners plenty to deal with when the weather changed.

Exterior

The Sprite retained a very simple level of exterior trim, which now included an aluminium radiator grille, replacing the chrome-plated steel grille of the Sprite Mk I. The Midget received a rather complexly constructed, vertical-slatted grille, which incorporated an MG badge. Side waistline trim strips and a central bonnet moulding were responsible for most of the additional cost. The Sprite retained the 'AH'-embossed, chromed hub caps, while the Midget received plain chrome hub caps. The chromed front bumper with over-riders was now standard equipment. Initially, the Sprite Mk I rear over-riders could still be fitted to reduce cost, but soon gave way to a full chrome rear bumper with over-riders.

Weather Equipment

The soft-top frame was now split in the centre; this allowed the frame to be stowed in the boot rather than behind the seats. As the cockpit was now effectively longer than the Sprite Mk I, a tonneau rail was introduced to fit into the soft-top frame sockets to support the longer span of the tonneau cover. The cover could now be folded over the rail and fastened to the heel panel behind the seats. Again, a central zip allowed the driver to keep the passenger side covered when travelling alone.

The factory option hard top for the Midget Mk I was alone in requiring revised side screens with a reverse angle to the trailing edge. This idea was soon dropped. (John Davies)

Andy Cross deliberates whether the optional anti-roll bar and after-market roll over bar might have been a good idea at Gurston Down Hill Climb.

Factory Options

The BMC dealerships had their own list of 'showroom' accessories to offer all their customers: seat covers, wing mirrors, fire extinguishers, wheel trims – no opportunity for an additional sale was missed. As before, DHMC and the BMC Tuning Department could offer a huge range of serious performance equipment for the more enthusiastic owner. However, the factory options list was as follows:

Laminated windscreen
Heater/blower unit
Fresh air unit (Hot climate option, essentially, the heater box without a matrix)
Tonneau cover and support rail
Hard top
Wire wheels (after October 1962)
Six-ply tyres
Whitewall tyres
Front anti-roll bar (from January 1964)
Rear compartment cushion

Original Colour Options for Sprite HAN6

Body colour	Seats and trim	Soft top	Tonneau	Hard top
Black	Cherry Red (to Feb. '62) Bright Red (from Feb. '62)	Grey	Red	Grey or Old English White (OEW)
Speedwell Blue (to Sep. '61)	Blue	Blue	Blue	Blue or OEW

Iris Blue (from Sep. '61)	Blue	Blue	Blue	Blue or OEW
Deep Pink	Black	Black	Black	Grey or OEW
Signal Red	Black or Red	Black	Black or Red	Red or OEW
Old English White	Black or Red	Grey	Black or Red	Red Grey Blue or OEW
Highway Yellow	Black	Black	Black	Grey or OEW

Original colour options for Midget GAN1

Body colour	**Seats and trim**	**Soft top**	**Tonneau**	**Hard top**
Black	Red	Grey	Red	Grey or OEW
Clipper Blue (to Sep. '61)	Blue	Blue	Blue	Blue or OEW
Ice Blue (from Sep. '61)	Blue	Blue	Blue	Blue or OEW
Almond Green (only used on 12 cars)	Green	Grey	Black	OEW
Farina Grey (to Sep. '61)	Red	Grey	Red	Grey or OEW
Dove Grey (from Sep. '61)	Red	Grey	Red	Grey or OEW
Tartan Red	Red or Black	Red	Black or Red	Red or OEW
Old English White	Black or Red	Grey	Black or Red	Grey or OEW

Original Colour Options for Sprite HAN7

Body colour	Seats and trim	Soft top	Tonneau	Hard top
Black	Red or Hazelnut	Black or Hazelnut		Grey or OEW
Iris Blue	Blue	Blue	Blue	Blue or OEW
British Racing Green (BRG)	Black	Black	Black	OEW
Dove Grey	Red	Grey	Red	Red or OEW
Signal Red	Red or Black	Red	Red	Red or OEW
Old English White	Hazelnut, Red or Black	Hazelnut Grey or Black	Hazelnut Red or Black	OEW
Fiesta Yellow	Black	Black	Black	OEW

Original Colour Options for Midget GAN2

Body colour	Seats and trim	Soft top	Tonneau	Hard top
Black	Red	Black	Black	Grey or OEW
Iris Blue	Blue	Blue	Blue	Blue or OEW
British Racing Green	Black or Hazelnut	Black or Hazelnut		OEW
Dove Grey	Red	Grey	Red	Grey or OEW
Tartan Red	Red or Black	Red	Red	Red or OEW
Old English White	Hazelnut Red or Black	Hazelnut Grey or Black	Hazelnvut Red or Black	OEW

5

The Sprite Mk III & Midget Mk II

October 1962 saw the introduction of the Triumph Spitfire. Triumph had the advantage of being able to study the previous Spridgets and then raise the benchmark. The Spitfire came with exterior, lockable door handles, winding side windows and larger cockpit with longer doors to ease access. However, it stuck to the old tradition by having the body mounted on a separate chassis. In March 1964, BMC addressed this challenge with the Sprite Mk III and Midget Mk II versions. The doors now also included lockable exterior door handles, winding windows and swivelling quarter light windows; however, the doors remained the same length, so access was not improved. Cockpit space, if anything, was slightly reduced by the thicker doors encroaching on elbow room. A new dashboard and instruments, sprung spoke steering wheel and a small parcel shelf on the passenger side were further revisions to counter the competition. The soft top now had a header rail, which was secured to a revised windscreen frame by two internal clamps. A much-improved 1098cc engine now had a recirculatory crankcase breather system. The quarter-elliptic rear springs were replaced by semi-elliptic springs, which offered an improved ride. Arguments may still exist as to whether the new type of rear spring offered better handling but, without doubt, the ride comfort was much improved. From the exterior, there was little to identify the new versions other than the doors, windscreen frame and a steeper rake to the soft-top rear window. During the production period, Midget sales began to exceed Sprite sales for the first time – a trend that would increase.

Other than a change of windscreen frame and exterior door handles, the much-revised Midget Mk II in this view conceals the majority of the revisions introduced from March 1964.

The centre bonnet trim moulding and side waistline trim strips are frequently lost features of the Midget Mk II, following a major body restoration. The Sprite Mk III did not have these cosmetic additions.

Model identification

VIN allocation	Number built
Sprite Mk III – HAN8/38829 to HAN8/64734	25,905
Midget Mk II – GAN3/25825 to GAN3/52389	26,601

The Body Unit

The door pillars and scuttle were revised to accept the new doors and windscreen frame. The B post was also revised to accept the new locking plate for the doors. Subtle changes to the shaping of the rear wings, where these blended into the B post, were also included. A bracket for the new rear spring shackle was added under the boot floor, a corresponding strengthening gusset being added to the inside of the boot to distribute the loading into the adjacent frame rail. The spring mounting box in the rear bulkhead was also modified to accept the new spring. The bracket for the now-redundant upper radius arm was deleted. Seat-belt mounting points were added for the 1965 model year.

Revised doors with wind-up windows, quarter lights and exterior lockable handles were all improvements, but came at the loss of the door pockets and some elbow room.

The latest version of the 1098cc engine now contained a Smiths crankcase recirculatory valve to direct engine venting into the inlet manifold.

Engine

Remaining at 1098cc, the engine received a number of improvements. A new crankshaft had larger-diameter main bearings, increased from a 1.875-inch to a 2-inch diameter. A revised cylinder block deleted the mechanical fuel pump aperture. Power output was now raised to 59 bhp. The new engine could be recognised by the prefix '10CC-DA-H' (or 'L' for low compression). The front tappet cover was revised to provide the connection to a closed-circuit breather system.

Fuel & Exhaust System

The mechanical fuel pump was now replaced by an electric SU pump located just in front of the rear axle on the right-hand side. A Smiths closed-circuit valve was now fitted to the inlet manifold to re-circulate crankcase vapours into the inlet manifold. The ventilation pipe between the rocker cover and front air-filter casing were deleted. A new oil filler cap containing a breather was fitted. A new, improved-shape cast-iron exhaust manifold was mated to an increased 1.5-inch-diameter exhaust system.

Gearbox & Clutch

The 7.25-inch-diameter clutch was retained, along with the previous gearbox. From April 1964, the gear tooth profile was revised but gear ratios remained unchanged.

Front Suspension & Steering

These were carried over from the previous versions.

Rear Axle & Suspension

The rear axle was now revised to accept the new, semi-elliptic spring mounting point. As before, a narrower unit would be fitted for the wire wheel option. The ratio remained at 4.22:1. The new springs required a revised front location box within the rear bulkhead and shackle locations beneath the boot floor.

Brakes

These were carried over from the previous versions.

Wheels & Tyres

These were not altered, other than to change to a coarser 8TPI thread for the hubs and spinners for the wire-wheel option. 'Eared' hub spinners were replaced by octagonal nuts for the safety-conscious North American market. The Sprite retained the chromed 'AH'-hub embossed caps for the steel disc wheels.

Electrics

Other than the required revisions for the new dashboard layout, as before.

Interior & Instruments

A completely revised dashboard contained redistributed instruments and switch gear. Information and function remained as before except for the addition of a blocked-oil-filter

Despite the Midget boasting additional exterior trim to the Sprite, it came with plain rather than embossed chrome hub caps. Why the Midget did not have MG-embossed hub caps to counter the AH hub caps of the Sprite is subject to further research.

The dashboard was now painted crackle black for all colour options. A spring-spoke steering wheel with central horn-push and a column-mounted, self-cancelling indicator stalk. A small parcel shelf was now provided in front of the passenger. A central dash-mounted badge identified SPRITE or a winged MG logo for the Midget. The Sprite grab handle was no longer provided for the passenger.

A foot-operated dipswitch, next to the clutch pedal, served until October 1969. The black rubber blanking piece alongside the clutch pedal gave access to the clutch slave cylinder bleed nipple. Above this, a hinged letter box flap controlled the air distribution to the footwell.

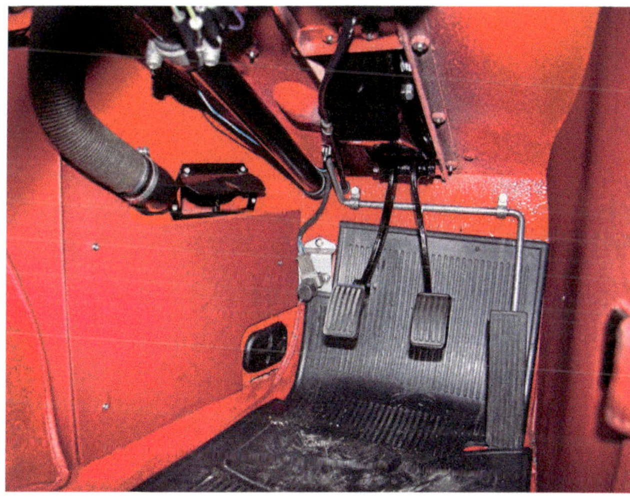

A new windscreen frame provided an easier and more positive fastening for the soft top. The removable tonneau cover support rail behind the seats allowed the cover to be folded and secured behind the seats as required. Additional leg room to utilise the optional rear seat cushion was not provided.

warning light above the oil-pressure/water-temperature gauge. Direction indicators now became self-cancelling, and were operated by a stalk control on the steering column. An optional headlamp flash was also operated by this control. The dashboard was now finished in wrinkle black paint instead of colour coded vynide. A small parcel shelf was added in front of the passenger. The ignition key now operated the starter motor via a solenoid. A new spring spoke steering wheel with central horn push boss completed the new look.

Improved, thicker padded seats with new covers were introduced in August 1965.

Exterior

The doors now sported chromed exterior handles, swivelling quarter lights and winding windows. A new windscreen frame provided an anchorage point for the new soft-top header rail and internal securing clamps.

Weather Equipment

A new soft top was provided with a header rail to secure to the windscreen frame via two internal clamps. This eased the operation of securing and releasing the soft top at the front but, otherwise, all the other attachments and stowage arrangements were as tedious as before!

Factory Options

Laminated windscreen
Heater/bower unit
Fresh air unit
Tonneau cover
Hard top
Wire wheels
Six ply tyres
Radial ply tyres (145X13)
Whitewall tyres
Front anti-roll bar
Headlamp flasher/indicator control
Oil cooler (From June 1965)
Rear compartment cushion

Original Colour Options

Body colour	Seats and trim	Soft top	Tonneau	Hardtop
Black	Black or Red	Black	Black	Black
Riviera Blue	Blue	Blue	Blue	Blue
British Racing Green	Black	Black	Black	Black
Dove Grey	Red	Grey	Red	Black
Tartan Red	Red or Black	Red or Black	Red or Black	Red or Black
Old English White	Black or Red	Black or Grey	Black or Red	OEW
Fiesta Yellow (to late 1965)	Black	Black	Black	Black
Pale Primrose (from late 1965)	Black	Black	Black	Black

Factory-optional hard top now included a rear quarter window. Again, the aftermarket industry could offer many alternative styles.

6

The Sprite Mk IV & Midget Mk III

Announced in October 1966, the Sprite Mk IV and Midget Mk III featured the much-anticipated 1275cc engine. Alas, it was not to the same specification as the Mini Cooper S for which many may have hoped. At a quoted 65 bhp, some 10 bhp less than the Cooper S, the new engine offered a useful increase over the previous 1098cc engine. However, the launch was not a smooth one; the initial 900 cars had to be held back due to an engine fault, which precluded deliveries to customers until 1967, when rectified engines became available. The soft top was much improved and no longer had to be removed and stowed in the boot. The rear edge of the cockpit was extended rearwards to allow room for the soft top to fold down behind the seats on a new folding frame. This was a very

The early Sprite MK IV in this view is indistinguishable from the previous MK III version. Only the extension of the rear cockpit edge and resulting gentler slope to the rear of the soft top would give any external clue to this being a 1275cc version. Additional driving lights are a popular modification.

An early Midget Mk III with the owner addition of a padded roll-over bar. A popular choice for safety-aware owners. Again, the popular swap to alloy wheels.

good arrangement and was retained until the end of production in 1979. From 1967, North American regulations demanded significant changes to be made; no longer could BMC just build a left-hand drive version of the home-market Spridgets.

Model Identification

VIN allocation		Number built
Sprite Mk IV	HAN9/64735 to 85286	20,357
Sprite Mk IV (Facelift)	HAN10/85387 to 86802	1,411
Austin Sprite	AAN10/86803 to 87824	1,022
Midget Mk III	GAN4/52390 to 74885	22,415
Midget Mk III (Facelift)	GAN5/74886 to 105146	29,544
Midget Mk III (Round arch)	GAN5/105501 to 153920	48,287

The Body Unit

The rear edge of the cockpit was extended rearwards by 4 inches to allow a revised soft-top arrangement to fold into the space behind the seats. The soft-top frame was now bolted to the tops of the B posts. The aperture for the master-cylinder pedal box was revised to allow the fitting of a new pedal box, containing separate brake and clutch master cylinders. From November 1967, the body unit for the North American market required numerous revisions to comply with forthcoming safety and emission regulations.

Engine

The new 1275cc engine produced 65 bhp at 6,000 rpm. The initial batch of these engines was found to have crankshaft and lubrication problems, which halted production until improved units could be supplied. It was not until early 1967 that customer deliveries properly began. To overcome this early problem, BMC produced crankshafts in EN40B steel, as used in the Mini Cooper S engine. This was an expensive part to manufacture.

The extended rear edge of the cockpit allowed the folding soft top and support frame to neatly be stored under this stowage cover.

The 1275cc engine provided 65 bhp and a useful increase in torque. Still a very recognisable descendant of the earlier 948 and 1098cc versions. This proved a very responsive engine to further tuning.

An alloy rocker cover and a change of air filters typify the modifications made by many owners to personalise the engine compartment. If you really want to be different, leave it as it came out of the factory!

From early 1968, a revised 1275cc engine was introduced with a stronger cylinder block; this would allow a change to a more cost-effective crankshaft made from EN16T. The stronger cylinder block can be identified by the change in engine prefix from '12CC' to '12CE'. The later engine had a thicker sump mounting flange and was now painted a lighter shade of green. Not that the change in colour added any additional strength of course!

Fuel & Exhaust System

This was carried over from the previous versions but with slightly reshaped air filter casings to allow for a reduced clearance to the bonnet. The engine was slightly taller than the previous 1098cc unit. From November 1967, North American versions received emission-control equipment. All fuel and crankcase venting would be recirculated or captured in carbon-absorption canisters. The twin 1.25-inch SU HS2 remained but was updated several times during production to comply with the changing regulations.

Gearbox & Clutch

The gearbox was carried over from the previous versions; the gear lever was now finished in black to replace the chrome lever. A reversing light switch was incorporated in the extension housing from September 1967 (HAN9/70268 and GAN4/58112). The 1275cc engine carried a 6.5-inch-diameter diaphragm clutch operated by a larger-diameter hydraulic slave cylinder and a new clutch master cylinder.

Front Suspension & Steering

This was carried over from the previous versions. The rack and pinion unit was changed from the Morris Minor-sourced unit to a Triumph-sourced unit from January 1972.

Rear Axle & Suspension

Carried over from the previous model – the crown wheel and pinion ratio was changed from 4.22:1 to 3.9:1 from December 1968.

Brakes

These were carried over from the previous version but were now operated by a dedicated master cylinder in a new pedal box. A dual-circuit hydraulic system was introduced for North American versions from November 1967 (HAN9/72034 and GAN4/60441).

Wheels & Tyres

For the HAN9/GAN4 versions, the steel-disc and wire-wheel options were carried over from before. For the facelift HAN10/GAN5 versions, the steel-disc wheels were replaced with the Rubery Owen Rostyle wheel of 13 inches by 4.5 inches. A second generation of the Rostyle wheel was introduced for the Round Arch Midget. The wire-wheel option remained but eared spinners were replaced by octagonal nuts for the home market during 1968. About this time, the option of radial ply tyres became standard issue.

One of the most common items for owners to change is the type of road wheel. The original steel disc wheels were plain; the Rostyle wheels, the second generation shown here, were regarded as too 'Ford Capri', while the wire wheels were time consuming to keep clean and suffered worn hubs.

Electrics

These were carried over from the previous model with a change to negative earth from November 1967 (HAN9/72041 and GAN4/60460). Alternators replaced the earlier dynamos from December 1972 (GAN5/128263) for the home market, which also removed the need for the voltage regulator box.

Interior & Instruments

Other than the extended cockpit, the Sprite HAN9 and Midget GAN4 remained unchanged for the home market. From November 1967, a padded fascia panel and revised instruments and controls were introduced for the North American market. The rev-counter red line was increased to 6,300 rpm from the 6,000 rpm of the 1098cc versions. The Facelift HAN10 and GAN5 versions received a revised interior trim pattern for the door liners and seats. There was a new simulated leather rim steering wheel and multi-function steering column stalk control. The gear lever now had a vynide gaiter over the steel cowl and rubber seal, while an ashtray was now provided, mounted to the tunnel behind the gear lever.

The dashboard was a continuation from the previous model; various minor changes occurred in later years. North American versions began to use a completely different layout to suit local safety regulations.

The sprung spoked steering wheel gave way to a simulated leather rimmed wheel with solid pierced spokes in October 1969. Despite looking a tad sportier, many owners still opted for something smaller, with a real leather rim.

The facelift of October 1969 essentially removed all the differences between the Sprite and Midget other than badging. Here, a rare Austin Sprite marks the final few months before Sprite production ceased in July 1971.

The facelift also introduced black finished sills for all colour options along with chrome-lettered script for Sprite or Midget – now the only identifier from the side view. The oblong B-L corporate badge on the lower rear edge of the wing was applied to all vehicles within the British-Leyland group.

Exterior

Other than the extended cockpit and the inclusion of twin reversing lights in the rear panel from September 1967, the Sprite HAN9 and Midget GAN4 retained the exterior of the previous versions. From December 1968, the Midget lost the centre bonnet moulding, and the front side light/indicator units were set lower in the wings for both Sprite and Midget. The Sprite HAN10 and Midget GAN5 were introduced in October 1969 as a facelift version. The Midget now lost the waistline trim strips and shared a revised version of the aluminium Sprite radiator grille. A thinner front bumper and quarter rear bumpers, revised badging and flatter rear light lenses added to a new look. The sills gained a trim strip but finished in black below the strip for all body-colour options. A Sprite or Midget script was added to the front of the sill panel. A new range of colours became available. From October 1971 (GAN5/105501), the rear wheel arches were reshaped to a round profile with a small flared edge.

Weather Equipment

A new convertible soft top was introduced that now made the raising and lowering operation a far easier proposition. The soft top was now permanently attached to the rear edge of an extended cockpit. A new folding frame allowed the soft top to lower into the space behind the seats, where it could be stowed under a fabric cover. The header rail from

The much-improved soft top led to fewer owners ordering hard tops. Here we see an aftermarket hard top on a facelift version.

The 'Round Arch' Midget was a final cosmetic update of the 1275cc version. Some argue that the rear wheel arches should have looked like this from the beginning. Cosmetic issues aside, the larger fuel tank was certainly a welcome feature.

the previous version was retained to secure the soft top to the windscreen frame. A longer tonneau cover was provided to span the extra 4 inches of cockpit length.

Options

Heater – Included as standard with the introduction of the facelift versions
Fresh air unit
Radio
Tonneau cover and rail
Laminated windscreen
Locking fuel cap
Wire wheels
Front anti-roll bar
Headlamp flasher
Oil cooler
Radial ply tyres (Became a standard fitment)
Whitewall tyres

Original Colour Options for Sprite HAN9 and Midget GAN3

The soft top, tonneau cover and hard top were now only available in black.

Body colour	Seat and trim
Black	Black or Red
Basilica Blue (to Nov. 1967)	Black
Mineral Blue (from Nov. 1967)	Black
British Racing Green	Black
Tartan Red	Red or Black (Red Midget only)
Old English White (to Nov. 1967)	Black or Red
Snowberry White (from Nov. 1967)	Black
Pale Primrose	Black

Original Colour Options for Sprite HAN10, AAN10 and Midget GAN5 (Facelift)

Body colour	Seat and trim
Black	Black
British Racing Green	Black (to Jun. 1970)
Glacier White	Black or Autumn Leaf (from Oct. 1969)
Bedouin	Black or Autumn Leaf (from Jun. 1970)
Pale Primrose	Black (to Jun. 1970)
Blaze	Black (from Jun. 1970)
Flame Red	Black (from Oct. 1969)
New Racing Green	Autumn Leaf (from Jun. 1970)
Blue Royale	Black (Oct. 1969 to Jun. 1970)
Midnight Blue	Black (from Jun. 1970)
Bronze Yellow	Black (from Oct. 1969)
Teal Blue	Black (from Jun. 1970)

Original Colour Options for Midget GAN5 with Round Rear Wheel Arches

Body colour	Seat and trim
Black	Navy (to Jul. 1972)
Bronze Yellow	Navy (to Aug. 1973)

Glacier White	Navy or Autumn Leaf
Blaze	Navy or Black
Flame Red	Navy (to Jul. 1972)
Teal Blue	Autumn Leaf or Ochre
Green Mallard	Autumn Leaf or Ochre (May 1971 to Aug. 1973)
Aqua	Navy (May 1971 to Jul. 1972)
Damask	Navy or Black
Harvest Gold	Navy or Black
Black Tulip	Navy or Black (from Jul. 1972) Ochre or Autumn Leaf
Limeflower	Navy (Jul. 1972 to Aug. 1973)
Mirage	Black (from Aug. 1973)
Bracken	Autumn Leaf (from Aug. 1973)
Aconite	Autumn Leaf (from Aug. 1973)
Citron	Black (from Aug. 1973)
Tundra	Autumn Leaf (from Aug. 1973)

7

The Midget 1500

To continue selling the Midget in the North American market, significant changes would now be required to meet the latest safety and emissions regulations. B-L had reached a point whereby they would either have to withdraw from the Midget's largest single market or meet the challenge with a completely new Midget. Instead, they decided to work with what they had. Their first problem was to meet the emission regulations, which now included the use of lead-free fuel. Rather than use the existing 1275cc A-Series engine, it was decided to use the 1493cc Triumph Spitfire engine. Once equipped with the full North American emissions package and with the overall increase in vehicle weight, the extra capacity would be essential to retain an acceptable level of performance. Furthermore, the Triumph engine came with hardened valve seat inserts in the cylinder head, something the A-Series engine never received in production. This would make the use of lead-free fuel a much easier proposition. To meet the latest low-speed impact without damage regulations, large, energy-absorbing bumpers were required, demanding substantial strengthening of the bumper mountings.

Left: The change to 'rubber' bumpers was dictated by regulations rather than a styling revision. Controversial at the time, some owners either remove or retro fit the earlier chrome bumpers, which is not as straight forward a job as it seems.

Right: At least the rear bumper provided somewhere to sit or tie shoe laces more easily, as subtle it most certainly was not.

Model Identification

VIN allocation: GAN6/154101 to 229526. **Number built:** 72,289

The Body Unit

Substantial revisions were required to mount the new, energy-absorbing bumpers, or 'Rubber Bumpers', as they are more commonly referred to. Additional box sections were added to each side of the engine compartment and boot floor to carry the mountings. The radiator surround assembly was now welded to the body unit. The rear wheel arches reverted to the previous square-topped profile. As the ride height would be increased to set the bumpers at the regulation height, the front wheel arches were produced 1 inch lower in the front wings. Further modifications to front and rear wings were required to accept the bumpers and to move the front indicator-light apertures.

Additional jacking points were provided at the rear of each sill. The floor pan now included an access aperture beneath the rear of the gearbox to allow access to the propeller shaft coupling.

Engine

Quite coincidently, the Triumph engine began life as an 803cc unit, the same capacity with which the BMC A-Series unit started life. The two engines trace their roots back to the early 1950s, both being stretched over the years to see service in a variety of applications before both finding a home in the Midget. The Triumph PE94/J engine featured an eight-port cylinder-head design but still a three bearing crankshaft. The cast-iron cylinder head and cylinder block was, again, a conventional four-cylinder overhead valve unit. For the home market, the power output was quoted as 65 bhp at 5,500 rpm, this being reduced by some 10 bhp for the emissions-control-equipped North American versions. Despite the same 65 bhp being quoted for both the home-market 1275cc and 1493cc engines, the performance of the heavier Midget 1500 was superior in terms of acceleration and top speed.

A deep-section frame rail was added to either side of the boot floor to support the new rear bumper.

Left: The 1493cc Triumph engine was a snug fit in the Midget engine compartment. Although of larger capacity with larger carburettors and an eight-port cylinder head, it was only accredited with the similar 65bhp output of the previous 1275cc engine.

Right: The 1493cc did not earn the best of reputations for longevity in service. Hence, few owners decide to tune these engines for more power. A careful rebuild and a sympathetic driver can help overcome this dubious reputation.

Fuel & Exhaust Systems

The fuel pump reverted to a mechanical AC unit to feed twin 1.5-inch SU HS4 carburettors. North American versions used a single 1.5-inch CD4 Zenith-Stromberg carburettor. A cast-iron exhaust manifold carried gasses away to a revised system with two-stage silencer boxes. From March 1975 (GAN6/160160), a catalyst was fitted below the manifold, initially for the Californian market only but subsequently for all North American versions from October 1975 (GAN6/166304).

Gearbox & Clutch

The cast-iron casing gearbox was sourced from the Morris Marina. This featured synchromesh on all four forward gears. The output shaft had a four-bolt flanged coupling to the front end of the propeller shaft. To access this coupling, for propeller shaft or gearbox removal, a square cut-out in the floor pan was provided. The hydraulically operated diaphragm clutch was 7.25 inches in diameter.

Front Suspension & Steering

This was carried over from the previous model but with longer coil springs to raise the ride height. For the home market, the front anti-roll bar was a standard fitment but was only an option on North American versions until December 1977 (GAN6/203341), when this became a standard fitment.

Rear Axle & Suspension

The rear axle was carried over from the previous version. The 3.9:1 crown wheel and pinion was replaced with a 3.77:1 unit from August 1977 (GAN6/200001) to take better advantage of higher torque characteristics of the larger engine. The handbrake mounting bracket on the axle was changed from August 1976 (GAN6/182001) to allow for a revised handbrake cable and linkage. The six-leaf rear springs were set to produce a raised ride height and a stiffer compression rate to cater for the increased weight.

Brakes

Front disc brakes remained unchanged. The rear wheel slave cylinder piston diameters were reduced to suit the increased weight distribution. For export markets, twin circuit hydraulic brakes had been included from 1968; from May 1978 (GAN6/212001) home-market Midgets now had this added safety feature as standard. The handbrake cable and linkage was revised in August 1976 (GAN6/182001).

Wheels & Tyres

The Rostlye steel wheel was carried over from before but the popularity of the wire wheel option had now declined. For the home market, the wire-wheel option was withdrawn in 1976 but remained for North America. 145 × 13 radial ply tyres remained the standard fitment.

The second-generation Rostyle wheel remained the standard fitment for the entire production life of the Midget 1500. Wire wheels became a less favourable option on the home market but were still quite popular for North America.

Electrics

The use of the Triumph engine required changes to the wiring loom to cater for the different positioning of electrical components. Further circuits were added as an increasing amount of emission and safety related components were incorporated.

Interior & Instruments

Trim was largely carried over from before, including the North American version. Seat belts became a standard fitment for the home market from April 1977.

Instruments were slightly revised but, from August 1977 (GAN6/200001), the Midget would now share the same instruments as the Triumph Spitfire. This saw the loss of the oil-pressure gauge, replaced by a warning light set in the speedometer.

While it was still the same basic dashboard from 1964, it incorporated many minor revisions along the way.

Instruments were changed in August 1977 to those from the Triumph Spitfire. This saw the loss of the oil-pressure gauge. The owner-fitted wood-rim steering wheel retains a link to an earlier period.

Exterior

The most obvious changes were the large black front and rear energy-absorbing 'rubber' bumpers, which were not made of rubber but a combination of polycarbonate over a polyurethane foam filling with a substantial steel armature. The rear bumper was nylon-covered to resist any fuel spillage. These were designed to withstand minor impacts without distortion, in line with the current North American regulations. The front bumper now incorporated the radiator grille surround and front indicator lights. Brightly finished trim strips were added to the lower rear wing quarters in line with the door sill strips and, similarly, the area below the strips finished in black.

Weather Equipment

This was carried over from the previous versions.

Home-market Factory Options

Head restraints	(Standardised for the home market from early 1977)
Wire wheels	(Until 1976)
Hard top	(Withdrawn at an undefined point)

The soft-top arrangement first appeared in late 1966; it proved good enough to remain virtually unchanged until the end of production in 1979.

In all black, the visual effect of the large front and rear bumpers is nicely blended in. The raised ride height is partly obscured by lowering the front wheel arch peak and reverting to square-topped rear wheel arches.

A sharp contrast between bumper and body colour accents the presence of the rubber bumpers. Here, the usual black-painted sill panels place a stronger emphasis on the body colour by removing the black link between front and rear.

Original colour options

Body colour	Seat and trim	All weather equipment in black only
Black	Black, Autumn Leaf or Beige	
Harvest Gold	Black (to Feb. 1976)	
Damask Red	Black (to Feb. 1976)	
Citron Yellow	Black (to Feb. 1976)	
Glacier White	Black or Autumn Leaf (to Aug. 1977)	
Bracken	Black or Autumn Leaf (to Feb. 1976)	
Tundra	Autumn Leaf (to Feb. 1976)	
Flamenco	Black (from around Feb. 1975 to Aug. 1977)	
Tahiti Blue	Black or Autumn Leaf (from around Feb. 1975 to Aug. 1977)	
Charttreuse Yellow	Black (from around Feb. 1976 to Aug. 1977)	
Sandglow	Autumn Leaf (from around Feb. 1976 to Aug. 1977)	
Brooklands Green	Autumn Leaf or Beige (from around Feb. 1976)	
Carmine Red	Black or Beige (from Feb. 1977)	
Leyland White	Black (Aug. 1977 to Jun. 1978)	
Inca Yellow	Black (from Aug. 1977)	
Vermillion	Black (from Aug. 1977)	
Pageant Blue	Beige (from Aug. 1977)	
Russet Brown	Beige (from Aug. 1977)	
Porcelain White	Black (from Jun. 1978)	

8

The Evolution Process

Back in 1958, neither Leonard Lord nor Donald Healey could have predicted a twenty-one-year production period for their new car. Many revisions were made during that period for a variety of reasons. However, all of the changes were evolutionary rather than revolutionary. Indeed, the more revolutionary changes that did reach prototype stage never went any further. Here, we look at the evolutionary process both during and after production.

Evolution by Design

Manufacturers must have an ongoing product-improvement programme. They cannot be seen to rest upon their laurels, and neither can they afford to. No matter how good their product when introduced, the need to improve is always there. Hence the Spridget became quicker, safer and more comfortable as the years progressed.

Evolution by Regulation

To produce a car, the manufacturer must meet the current regulations covering vehicle construction and operation. As most manufacturers need to export, worldwide regulations all have to be satisfied. During the twenty-one years of production, the regulations changed dramatically, resulting in many conformity revisions having to be made, led mostly by the North American market, which became very safety- and emissions-conscious in the later 1960s. This eventually led to North America-bound Midgets being considerably different, and slower, in comparison to the home-market examples. However, the effect of such changes did have some impact for the home-market versions.

Evolution within the Industry

Some changes are incorporated as the manufacturer may wish to reduce, standardise or improve component specifications. If components can be shared by other models in their product range, production parts and costs can be reduced. This is also true within the supply chain that provides products to the industry. Hence, components may be redesigned, constructed or produced differently or made of a different material. Whether to improve the component itself, reduce inventory or to reduce cost, these are the sorts of changes that the manufacturer may prefer to keep on a need-to-know basis only.

Evolution through Motorsport

From the very beginning, the Sprite proved itself to be a very competent motor sport contender. Be it circuit racing, rallying, hill climbing, trails, auto tests and sprinting, the Sprite – and the later Midget – proved a very formidable all-rounder. Both the DHMC and BMC's own Special Tuning and Competitions department have helped develop and provide equipment to peruse the motorsport aspect. This in itself is a huge and complex story and outside the scope of this book. Suffice to say that the competition career of the Spridgets have both attracted customers and helped in the development of the cars.

Evolution Learnt the Hard Way

Manufacturers also improve their products through lessons learned the hard way – mistakes! The manufacturer's nightmare – a product recall to rectify a fault – is costly, embarrassing and damaging. BMC issued a number of bulletins to dealerships to advise on the replacement of suspect components that could impair reliability or safety. For the Spridget, these were mostly of a minor nature but, nevertheless, quite a number of components had to be improved quietly to ensure that reliability and safety in service would not be compromised.

Evolution Continues

We have seen how the various evolutionary elements steered the changes during the twenty-one years of production. However, the process continues. Not long after production finished, a number of specialist companies was formed to provide spare parts and services to owners. Initially, redundant stock from the manufacturer and their suppliers was still available, but this was limited. Gradually, the specialists began to commission remanufactured components, either from original sources or, more so, from new ones. As interest in the cars began to re-emerge, more and more remanufactured parts were added to the catalogues. However, remanufactured parts may differ from original parts. This may be for a variety of reasons, such as expediency of production methods, costs, market demand and, sometimes, to provide an improved component to the original. This can work both ways, some remanufactured parts are not as good as an original item, the suppliers perhaps believing that today's owners will not subject their cars to the rigours of everyday usage.

While many minor components became available, a small company on the Isle of Wight took a major step. This was the Frogeye Car Company of Ryde. To save as many Frogeye

Sprites as possible, a complete new body unit to replace an otherwise unsalvageable Frogeye became available in 1986. However, this was a fibreglass body on a galvanised-steel-tube space frame chassis. Such was the quality of this alternative that Geoffrey Healey gave the project his endorsement to rename this product as the Healey Frogeye for the factory-assembled cars from 1989. Around 130 of these 'Isle of Wight' Frogeyes were built, either as a replacement for an original Sprite MK1 or to Healey Frogeye specification as a complete car. The final factory versions had a Rover K-series engine and five-speed gearbox.

Meanwhile, in 1991, the Rover Group, as successors to B-L, set up a new subsidiary, British Motor Heritage, to remanufacture complete steel body units for the MGB and MG Midget. From a new manufacturing plant in Farringdon near Oxford, BMH could supply a complete body unit for the 1275cc and 1500 versions. Due to the large number of revisions made during this production period, a commonised specification had to be adopted; hence the BMH body unit is not totally original to any one particular model-year. These body units are still available to order.

Such was the demand for original body units for the Sprite Mk1, an independent company, Wheeler Davis, began limited production; these are also still available from suppliers, Frogeye Spares.

Many owners now seek modified components to allow better usage and serviceability in modern-day driving conditions. The industry has responded magnificently on this aspect. Whether to run on unleaded fuel, improved braking, handling or a modern twin cam engine and five-speed gearbox, the options are endless and ongoing. Evolution does indeed continue.

9

Becoming an Owner

Essentially, there are two sorts of potential new owner: firstly, someone who used to own one and would now like to recapture the memories and joys of an earlier life; secondly, someone who has no previous experience of these cars, but can see the enjoyment that ownership can offer. In the first instance, the buyer may already have a very clear idea of which version to buy – perhaps the same colour as their previous Spridget. Previous knowledge and happy memories go a long way toward beginning the search to recapture those days.

Finding the right one requires patience, knowledge and willingness to travel: once found, proceed without delay before someone else snaps it up.

For our second group, then, it's time for research. First of all, try one. The doors are short and the seat is low – can you get in and out easily? Once in, can you get comfortable and handle the controls? Assuming that you are still smiling, then a test drive is essential, even if it is not the exact version that you may already have in mind. Driving a Spridget is not like driving any modern vehicle: there is no servo assistance; the ride is lively; everything is very direct. It may take some getting used to. If possible, try the car with the soft top both raised and lowered, as the contrast is considerable and you need to experience the difference. Only you can decide exactly which version you want, so be aware of the choice available and the considerable variations in asking price. The version, condition, specification and history all have an impact on values.

Next, do you want a restoration project or something to just use and have fun with – or is it all out originality and a sideboard awaiting some concours competition trophies? There is a world of difference, and cost, in deciding how you want to purchase and use any specific version. Restoration is not for everyone, any more than concours competitions are. You need to look at how you will use your Spridget and what level of modifications may be desirable to get it the way you want it in today's world. Understanding the differences that each version offers, along with the value and condition, is important. Generally, the later the version the more useable it is likely to be. For the versions prior to March 1964, the doors cannot be locked, the side windows are removable framed screens, the quarter-elliptic rear suspension is hard and the soft top takes time and practice to operate. From 1964, lockable doors with winding glass windows, much-improved operation and stowage of the soft top,

Ensure that you can enter and exit the car easily; small doors and close-to-the-ground seating may prove challenging for some. Check this with the soft top raised or hard top fitted, too, both of which add to the challenge. Once in, ensure you have room to handle all the controls safely. Although the driver seat is adjustable for reach, most find that fully back is required. Even so, many 6-foot-tall owners are quite comfortable.

and more power from larger engines all marked the progress of the Spridget into a more user-friendly and safer world.

Once you have decided on which version would be best for you, how do you want it?

Buying to Restore

Restoring is often underestimated in terms of time, cost and frustration. Experienced restorers can sometimes make this sound easy, but for the first timer – beware. An already stripped or partially restored example is risky: is everything there? Do all those boxes of bits add up to a complete car? Even if they do, remember it was someone else who did the deed and ask yourself if you would know if all the bits were there or even if they were all the correct bits? Moreover, would you know how to recognise and where to replace all those items? Careful restorers will bag, label, photograph and record every single item.

An abandoned restoration also raises the question, why was it abandoned? Did the restoration go horribly wrong? Was the body unit welded only to find that the doors no longer fit or some other misalignment discovered? What is the quality of any work done? Trying to undo and correct the mistakes of others can be a lot more difficult than beginning with a ropey but unmolested example. It is far better to buy a complete car so that you can see that it is all there. If restoration is your objective, having suitable working and storage areas must be considered, as this will not be a job to do in your open driveway on a Sunday afternoon when the sun shines. If restoration is your thing, then these cars are eminently suitable. They are simply constructed; parts supply is good; and there is always plenty of good advice from the owners' clubs.

Be aware, however, that the cost of a full restoration, especially if contracting out work, can easily exceed the ultimate value of the car.

Buying One You Can Use

Buying a useable example is a much easier proposition. Remember, virtually all examples today will have had major work carried out in the past, but how well has this work been done? Invoices, photograph albums and documentation of work carried out are essential clues. Invoices and documentation should contain dates and costs in addition to what has been done and who may have provided parts and services in the past. In additional to checking the general condition, checking for correct specification is also important. Has the car been modified intentionally or just repaired with any handy item that could be sourced at the time? Some modifications are desirable, especially some period accessories, but non-original features that were only fitted as an easy or cheap repair can devalue the car or even compromise its reliability and safety.

Buying a top-rung version to original condition and specification will come at a top-rung price. You have to ensure that it is top rung. Here, you need to do your homework meticulously and you will need an expert pair of eyes with you. If originality is of high priority, you really do need to know the version intimately. Any slight deviations or imperfections have to be spotted. Viewing will take time, even if you do know the car and the vendor. This is the specialised end of ownership and the most demanding; get it right, and it can also be the best long-term value for money option too.

We now look at the practical side of buying a Spridget and what to look for.

Where to Look

The owners' clubs, the classic car magazines and the internet are all good starting points. Be prepared to travel, as the right car for you may not be in the right place. As well as setting your budget, set a time and distance as to how far you are prepared to go. Also, take into consideration the viewing conditions: viewing in the dark, pouring rain, freezing cold or with an insufficient time allowance all have to be avoided. Check with the vendor about the viewing facilities, and find out whether this will be in a well-lit, heated and spacious showroom, or on the side of a road under an umbrella? Specialist dealerships should not be ruled out, even though the asking price may be higher. Dealerships have a reputation to maintain and a legal obligation to customers that a private seller does not. However, a dealership may not have the intimate knowledge of a particular example that a long-term owner would have.

Viewing

Ensure you have made a firm appointment with the vendor as to when and where to view the car. You don't need to be making a long journey only to discover the car has been sold, the vendor has forgotten or some other minor issue prevents your purpose. Conversely, inform the vendor if you are likely to arrive late or have decided not to view their car. Take along another pair of eyes to help spot anything that you may overlook, especially if the vendor attempts to distract your viewing process by irrelevant chatter or endless cups of tea: concentrate on the matter in hand. If you have little or zero previous experience of these cars, join an owners' club. You may find they have an expert nearby who could offer some invaluable help. The owners' clubs may already know both the car and vendor. Take along some overalls and a jack for looking underneath. A torch, gloves, proof of insurance for a test drive and, of course, the means to pay should it be the right one for you.

Documentation

Always start here, even when the temptation to get behind the steering wheel is beckoning. Check firstly the registration documents to see if all the ID marks and ownership details agree with the vehicle and the vendor. The VIN prefix will identify the version you should be viewing: is this example a jumbled collection of parts from other versions? Invoices, historical documentation and photographs will provide an important clue to what you are about to view. Do the invoices actually apply to this car or are they just added to the collection for effect?

The Vendor

Is the owner conversant with the car? You should be summing up the seller as well as the car at this stage. Find out how long have they owned it, whether they have carried out any work and why are they selling it. Are they a member of an owners' club? Are they selling it on behalf of someone else? Asking the seller for fuel and oil consumption figures or when the last service was carried out should provide quick and clear answers. Is the seller a genuine enthusiast, or someone trying to make a profit or trying to unload a liability? You need to find out.

A Test Drive

Firstly, you must be insured to drive someone else's vehicle and the vendor may ask for proof of this. A vendor may also be reluctant to let just anybody drive their car, so be prepared to have to make judgement from the passenger seat if you fail to gain the confidence of the vendor. It is vital to take a drive with the soft top both raised and lowered. Wind noise will drown out many nasty noises such as bearing rumbles, transmission noises, suspension clonks, or squeaks and rattles. Even if it is the hottest of days, you must sample a drive with the soft top raised.

A thorough test drive is essential; here, the 'wet feet' test is being performed. It passed!

Body Unit

Rust and accident damage are the main enemies here. Replacing rusty panels is achievable, but a major accident may have pushed the body unit out of alignment and may prove impossible to correct. Check the front cross members and the frame rails either side. Any wrinkling, unusual welds, creasing or splits in this region are warning signs. The underside of the cross member will almost certainly be dented upwards. This is due to careless jacking up of the vehicle. A load-spreading packing piece should always be used when jacking under the cross member; the centre is an unsupported steel panel and is not designed to take the weight of the vehicle. While viewing the underside from the front, note that the frame rails either side of the engine are designed to be curved upwards. This is not accident damage although it may look that way. Other than this curvature, again, check these rails for any sign of damage that may have been caused by a heavy front-end impact or heavy grounding. Check the boot floor for any signs of a rear-end collision: any wrinkles to the floor or side frame rails are danger signs. The very rear edge of the floor is susceptible to rust, so any welded repairs here may be nothing more than just this. The important check is the external panel fit, especially around the doors. The door gaps should be constant and even, as any paint scrapes, resistance to open and close cleanly may indicate that the door gap is incorrect. This is often the case when the body unit has not been properly supported and aligned when replacement sills have been fitted. Although not accident damage, to correct this is a major job. All other panel gaps should again be constant and even, the exception being the fit of the Sprite Mk I bonnet, which is often less than perfect. This has always been very difficult to achieve, even when the Sprite was new. Check carefully around the spring mounting area; the rear bulkhead is a highly stressed area made up of enclosed box sections, which can harbour moisture and rust from the inside. If a quarter-elliptic spring version, check that the thick mounting plate below the spring is parallel to the bottom edge of the sill: if it is higher at the rear, then the spring mounting has moved due to weakening of the spring location and surrounding area. This can be a major job to correct. If possible, lift all the carpeting to check the inside of the floor and rear bulkhead; floors do get wet and rust can spread unseen beneath the floor coverings.

Engine

Is it the correct engine and, if not, what is it? Check the oil pressure on start-up: the gauge should give an immediate reading and rise to around 60 lbs at idle when cold or 25 lbs minimum at idle when hot. Normal running pressure when hot is around 60 lbs. Listen for signs of any bearing rumble. The timing chain can rattle on the pre-1275cc engine versions that used a single-row timing chain. This is less likely with the twin row timing chain of the 1275cc engine but listen for noise anyway. Blue smoke from the exhaust may be just a malfunctioning breather system but be suspicious of worn valve guides or cylinder bores and piston rings. Oil leakage is common on these engines, so check beneath for drips or even puddles. Valve-gear rattle is not unusual but should not be excessive. A worn rocker shaft and rockers or just poor adjustment may be the cause but a worn camshaft and tappets will be an engine removal job to fix. The 1493cc engine has a reputation for short

The A-series engine is usually a robust unit, but can become noisy, leak and burn oil when worn. Check oil pressure, oil drips and exhaust for blue smoke.

The 1493cc Triumph engine is known to suffer bearing problems. Check the crankshaft for end float in additional to all the usual noise and visual checks.

main bearing life, so check for crankshaft end float and deep rumblings from within. Has the engine been properly modified to run on unleaded fuel? Don't just take the vendor's word for it, and ask for documented proof of this. Indeed, any claimed modifications to the engine should be accompanied by some proof.

Gearbox

All the A-Series engine gearboxes will whine in the non-synchromesh first gear. A rattle in first gear will mean a worn lay shaft and bearings. This will be an expensive fix. Check that all gears engage quietly and that none jump out of engagement under power or over-run. The Midget 1500 is generally a reliable and quiet unit.

The front suspension does require regular lubrication to avoid advance wear. A complete rebuild is fairly simple but costly and avoidable for those prepared to spend a few minutes with a grease gun.

Front Suspension & Steering

Regular greasing of the front suspension kingpins, fulcrum pin and track rod ends is vital to resist rapid wear and the ingress of moisture. Although replacement components are readily available, a complete rebuild will be costly. The front lever arm dampers also form the upper suspension link. This dual role can also spell double trouble; this single item must continue to perform both tasks properly or handling and ride will be compromised. A conversion kit to replace the lever arm damper with a telescopic damper and a new upper arm and bearing unit is a popular alternative. The rack and pinion unit is a reliable and long-lasting unit; as long as the rubber end gaiters are leak free, it provides very accurate and light steering input.

Rear Axle & Suspension

Rear springs can settle with age and result in a reduced ride height, so look for distortion in the curvature of the springs and for broken or cracked leaves. Clamps around the leaf bundle hold the spring together; these can break and lose grip, causing the leaves to separate. Most importantly, a low ride height may be due to corrosion around the spring mounting points, necessitating extensive body-unit repairs. The rear dampers need to be checked for leakage but ensure that any oil found has not resulted from being deposited by a leaking differential input shaft oil seal flinging oil onto the dampers.

Both the quarter-elliptic and semi-elliptic rear springs, as here, are prone to sagging and breakage. Regular inspection and lubricating is advisable. The rear lever arm dampers are much longer lived than the front units. A conversion to telescopic rear dampers is available.

Brakes

Compared to modern vehicles, braking performance is modest, especially with the front drum braked versions. However, the handbrake should be very effective. Brakes should pull up without pulling to one side or judder. The pedal requires more effort than modern, servo-assisted cars, but not unduly so. The happy news is that the braking system is very simple and easy to work on, should it be required. Check the level and condition of the brake fluid in the master cylinder. Many earlier, front drum brake versions have the later disc brake fitted; however, to do this correctly, the master and rear wheel slave cylinders should also have been changed at the same time. Any mismatch of braking components can cause excessive pedal travel or an imbalanced system.

Disc front brakes became standard from October 1962 and have proved a popular retro fit to earlier examples. Even so, by today's standards, the standard disc front and drum rear brakes are rather mediocre in performance.

Cosmetic refurbishment can be tedious, especially the complex, sculptured form of the Rostyle wheels. Wire wheels require specialist restoration and may require new splined hubs to be fitted to the car as well. Hence, so many owners now opt for alloy wheels instead.

Wheels & Tyres

Both steel-disc and wire wheels can suffer cosmetically as rust eventually appears through the paintwork. Although this can be remedied, rim damage caused by kerbing or pot holes cannot. Wire wheels also suffer loose spokes and running out of true. A clicking sound when braking or accelerating may indicate loose hub nuts or, more seriously, worn hub splines. Both wheel and car hubs need to be replaced to cure this. An expensive job.

Electric

Check that all the electrical functions work and that the wiring is tidy and undamaged. Previous owners fitting additions to the electrical system can sometimes make a mess of things. The Lucas system should be reliable, with either a dynamo and control box or alternator systems. The most difficult item to change is the main wiring loom; most other components can be easily changed if necessary.

Interior & Instruments

Check that all the instruments are of the correct type for the version and operate correctly. With age, speedometers and rev counters can lose correct calibration and produce

The interiors of open cars can suffer quite badly and be a real put-off. Thankfully, the simple trim and availability of parts mean that refurbishment is quite feasible.

inaccurate readings. Instruments can be replaced, but at a cost. Interior trim and carpeting can suffer in any open car. A musty smell indicates that the carpets have become sponges. Fortunately, most of the interior trim is easy and fairly cheap to renew.

Exterior

Begin with the panel fit. Look for any uneven gap and shut lines, or for any dents or wrinkling in the panels. The panel joint seams attract corrosion and pretty much anything below the level of the windscreen, which is everything else! These cars can display corrosion damage on all of the steel panels. Inspect every inch of the bodywork for signs of repair. Operate the doors and locking, window operation, boot and bonnet lid fit and operation. Is all the exterior trim fitted in line with the version specification? You should know what should be there.

Poorly fitting panels can be very difficult to correct. Even if the paintwork is gleaming, avoid a car that displays uneven gap lines. Check the doors open and close properly, along with bonnet and boot lids.

The soft-top frame, particularly the later examples, must be free of distortion, sticking pivots and bent links. Check for correct operation carefully.

Weather Equipment

Check the fit and condition of the soft top and tonneau cover. Rips and tears are obvious, especially around the fasteners. It is important to check the operation of both as the material can shrink in time, making attachment a struggle. Check also the condition and operation of the tubular hood frame. The various pivots and spring-loaded sections can seize, while the tubes and links can distort. The removable side screens of the early versions have Perspex sliding panes that discolour, become scratched, and will certainly rattle within the aluminium frame. Check the surround rubbers and freedom of movement of the panes. Check that the stowage bags containing the weather equipment are present and in good condition. If a winding window version, check the operation, of both windows and quarterlights, as these are a fiddly job to repair.

Options, Accessories & Modifications

These are quite a minefield. Some optional extras and modifications can he highly desirable and add value; others, quite the opposite. Expert help may be required here to help identify what is being offered. Spridgets were 'personalised' by their owners almost from day one, and many days and owners have subsequently added their mark in either direction.

This highly modified example started life as a Midget 1500. A Frogeye bonnet and aerò windscreen are the tip of a long list of modifications to the owner's own personal requirements. Placing a value on such an unusual example sets it outside of the normal price guide.

What to Pay

The owners' clubs should be able to provide the best advice on the current real-world values: asking prices and selling prices can be very different. Most vendors will ask the top valuation-guide prices, even when their offering is not in the top-condition category. Some modifications and period accessories can add value, while others detract, so you need to know which way the pendulum swings with examples that do not conform to factory specification. Also, examples with an interesting history or of special historical significance can demand a higher price than the accepted. Expert advice is required when viewing something out of the ordinary. Depreciation is not a term applicable to these cars today; asking prices are rising, but at varying rates according to the version.

10

Ownership Today

Sprite and Midget come together for an end-to-end comparison test. We can declare it a draw for the opening bits!

Today, we live in a rather different world from the one that the Sprite and Midget were born into. But, as they live on, how does the owner of today cope with looking after their old four-wheeled friend?

In truth, the owner of today is rather different too. Originally aimed at a younger market on a restricted budget, today's owner is more likely to be a little further on in his or her motoring career. It may well not be their only car either; their Spridget may only come out w[illegible] sun shines or the mood takes. It is spared the rigours of daily commuting in all winds and weathers, being left outside, suffering skimped maintenance and an owner dreaming of the replacement car. Most Spridgets are well cared for and used sparingly by a far more caring and mature sort of owner. However, the fun factor has not diminished, and the following describes how the fun factor can be preserved and enjoyed today. We now look at the sort of changes, support, modifications and the ownership issues that keep the Spridgets on the road today.

Fuel

In the UK, leaded fuel disappeared from the forecourts in 1998, many years after the last Midget was built. None of the A-Series engines of the time were designed to run on unleaded fuel. The fitment of hardened valve seats along improved quality valves and guides can allow modern forecourt fuel to be used without fear of valve-seat recession. However, this is an expensive conversion and not always cost effective to do if the engine is otherwise in good condition or covers a low annual mileage. Instead, a suitable fuel additive can offer sufficient protection in an otherwise standard engine. It would be advisable to check the valve clearances more regularly to ensure that the gaps do not reduce. It should be noted that different brands of additive should not be mixed. Different chemical bases are used by different brands that may not be compatible. The Midget 1500 always had valve seat inserts

This much-modified Frogeye has a long-range fuel tank fitted with a repositioned filler cap. Many owners now fit an inline fuel filter between tank and engine to prevent debris from older fuel tanks reaching the carburettors.

The SU carburettors are very reliable and easy to refurbish when worn. Many owners are tempted to change these due to misinformation from less well-informed sources.

fitted, but a better-quality insert was used for North American versions when unleaded fuel was introduced there. Again, an additive should suffice until such time that the engine may need other work. If an engine is modified to increase performance and the regular use of high rpm, then hardened valve seats should be used. The increasing content of ethanol in petrol is now causing some concerns. Ethanol is hygroscopic and may affect corrosion resistance and combustion temperatures. Vapour locks may also occur in high-temperature conditions. Again, there are additives available that may help guard against some effects; otherwise, some modification and retuning of the engine settings may also be required.

Servicing

The service schedule for early versions advised a change of oil every 3,000 miles and a change of oil filter at alternate oil changes. Improved oils and fuels will allow a change of both at 5,000-mile intervals on a regularly used car. Otherwise, an annual change of both would be advisable. A grease gun is an essential part of the tool box, so don't be afraid to use it! The front suspension and steering should be greased at least annually – just before the MOT seems a favourite time! The use of silicone brake fluid is popular with owners who leave their car for long periods in storage. It is essential not to mix traditional hydraulic fluids with silicone fluids. A change from one to the other can only be achieved following a complete renewal of the hydraulic system.

Hydraulic systems for both brakes and clutch are very simple and reliable. Many owners who store their cars for long periods prefer to use silicone hydraulic fluid.

Modifications

From the very beginning, owners wanted to modify their cars in some way, with at least a different steering wheel or a pair of chromed air filters. There have been some sensible and some inept modifications performed by owners over the years. There is a word of warning before making any modification, however. Many owners are tempted to modify or upgrade a component simply because the old component has worn out. In many instances, just replacing old for new will be perfectly adequate. Some modifications may only work properly when performed with other changes to the original specification; hence, replacing one item may be stepping onto a long and twisting path of modifications, along with expense, that may be quite unnecessary. Here, it is essential to gain the experiences of

The DHMC offered a supercharger kit for the Sprite Mk I. Here, a modern supercharger kit is fitted to a Sprite Mk IV. The ancient art of bolting on a huge power increase can still be realised.

others when it comes to making such a step – join the club! Hence, we look at some of the sensible modifications that are popular with owners today.

Engine

The fitting of a larger-capacity A-Series engine has always been popular and, of course, simple too, as this does not involve irrevocable modifications to the body unit. Increasing the power output of any of the A-Series engines has also been a popular and well-trodden path. A huge amount of tuning equipment has been available over the years and that remains the case today. Tuning the 1493cc has never been so popular, due to the inherent bearing weakness of this engine. Changing to a more modern engine is an option on all versions, the most popular options today being the Rover K-Series or Ford Zetec engines. However, both of these involve modifications to the body unit.

The Rover K-series engine is proving a very popular alternative to the original BMC and Triumph engines. A kit is available to make this change but is expensive and requires quite a lot of work. Seen here in an Isle of Wight (Frogeye Car Company) example for clarity.

The Ford Zetec engine is also an option but, again, it is not a cheap or a weekend-swap job. Seen here in a special body (Stuart Taylor) Frogeye. If retaining the fuel-injection system and ECU of a modern engine, a lot needs to be transferred over. This Zetec is fitted with motorcycle carburettors.

Lubrication

Modern, synthetic oils are unsuitable for the A-Series or the 1493cc engines. These engines were designed when monograde oils were used, with a thin grade in winter and a thicker grade for summer use. Multi-grade oils became available, which can be used all year round; these are suitable for both engine types. Mineral-based, multi-grade oils of a suitable viscosity rating are tending to disappear from some sources but can still be obtained through the classic-car specialists. Note that the A-Series engine can develop oil leaks, especially from the rear main bearing. An oil-seal conversion kit is available to address this particular problem. Prior to October 1969, a replaceable oil filter element was contained within an outer housing. Changing the element can prove tricky and an oil leak on start-up is quite common and, potentially, damaging. After 1969, a screw-on replaceable oil filter was used, which overcame both problems. These can be used on the earlier versions, providing the filter head casting is changed; this is an easy and popular conversion. All the A-Series engines can be expected to use a little oil in service. 800 miles per pint of oil is not unreasonable but less that 500 will indicate a well-worn engine, and you can expect blue smoke from the exhaust at this stage. The crankcase breather systems changed over the years from atmospheric to fully recirculatory. It is important to maintain either system in good condition. Modified breather systems can be applied poorly by owners not

The BMC A-series engine is notorious for oil leaks. The engine breather system needs to be kept in good order, especially the early Smiths recirculator valve mounted on the inlet manifold. A split diaphragm can simulate a blown engine.

fully understanding the issues. An engine that suffers a poorly maintained, modified or blocked breather system may leak or burn excessive amounts of engine oil, due to excessive crankcase pressure.

Fuel System

The SU carburettors are simple and reliable. Refurbishment when worn is also simple. Many owners are tempted to change rather than refurbish worn carburettors. The more recent SU HIF series of carburettor, in single form, has proved popular but requires a new inlet manifold. The Weber DCOE carburettor has always been popular for higher power applications when more extensive modifications have been made. Although the original SU pump is usually reliable, this has often been replaced by a more modern alternative. The fitting of an in-line fuel filter is sensible where an old fuel tank, and infrequent use, may allow debris to reach the carburettors.

The twin SU carburettors require minimal attention when in good condition. When wear does take over, mostly in form of worn throttle spindles, metering needle, set and float chamber values, refurbishment is simple. Parts supply is excellent.

The Weber DCOE side draught carburettor has been a very popular performance option for many years. The more modern SU HIF series of carburettors provides a strong challenge to the traditional Weber when it comes to extracting the maximum. However, nothing compares to the Weber when it comes to the characteristic noise it makes!

A five-speed gearbox is a very popular swap but does leave the gear lever further back along the tunnel. Some cutting and squeezing of the body is required, and so may not attract owners unwilling to make irrevocable changes. Seen here in an Isle of Wight (Frogeye Car Company) Frogeye, which has a wider transmission tunnel than a standard steel body.

This Sprite has an over-drive unit from a Triumph Spitfire to give a six-speed transmission. The over-drive is controlled from a switch in the gear knob. Quite a popular modification before five-speed gearboxes became easily available. Now, over-drive units are becoming difficult to find.

Gearbox

The five-speed Ford Serria Type 9 gearbox is the most common one to use. Prior to this, a Toyota gearbox was favourite but has become in short supply in recent years, something that is now becoming a problem with the Type 9 gearbox. With either, a conversion kit of parts is commercially available. The Midget 1500 can also take advantage by using the Triumph Spitfire gearbox with the optional overdrive unit.

Ignition System

The fitting of an electronic ignition system to dispense with the traditional contact breaker system has proven popular with many owners. In practice, if the original system is in good order, then it is both reliable and simple to service. A change of engine will require the compatible ignition or engine management system to be fitted.

A very popular modification to the front suspension from Frontline. The lever arm damper is replaced by a fabricated top arm/bearing assembly and a modern telescopic damper incorporated.

Front Suspension & Steering

The replacement of the lever arm front dampers by telescopic dampers has proven very popular. Frontline Spridget have offered a conversion kit for this from the 1980s. Stiffer rate and lowered front coil springs are also available, alongside different-diameter anti-roll bars.

Rear Axle & Suspension

Over the years, various crown wheel and pinion ratios of 4.22, 3.9 and 3.7:1 have been used, all are interchangeable within the rear axle. With an increase in engine size or power, fitting a higher ratio is easily accomplished. Fitting a five-speed gearbox or an overdrive gearbox for the Midget 1500 will also extend the cruising ability. A telescopic rear damper conversion kit is a long-established option. Anti-tramp bars to improve lateral location and a panhard rod to improve transverse location of the axle are available. These are more appropriate for a substantial increase in engine power or motorsport application. Double bearing rear hubs offer better half-shaft support for motor sport applications. Early steel wheel half shafts were prone to breakage, and a better half shaft was introduced that cured the problem; look for the part number 'BTA 806' on the visible end of the improved half shaft. For handling substantial increases in power or for competition, then up-rated half shafts are available from specialist suppliers.

Brakes

Owners of early drum front braked versions often upgrade to the later disc front brake specification. A remote brake servo unit may also be fitted to reduce pedal load. Improved front brake pad materials, front callipers or larger-diameter disc brake conversions are commercially available. If fitting different brakes, then a change of master cylinder or slave cylinder may be required to balance the hydraulic system properly. The flexible rubber hoses can be replaced with braided hoses; if changing the type of hose, always check that the front wheels clear the hose on full steering lock and that the hose does not become trapped with any part of the suspension or body.

Wire wheels became a factory option and really look the part. In reality, keeping clean and hub spline wear meant that many owners converted to aftermarket alloy wheels. Original wire wheels were painted; chromed wire wheels are an aftermarket option. Eared spinners gave way to octagonal nuts for safety reasons.

Wheels & Tyres

Today, the fitment of alloy wheels seems to be the most popular of all modifications, especially the traditional Minilite pattern wheel. The traditional wire wheel, although looking absolutely in keeping, provided maintenance problems in service as well as being time consuming to keep clean; this tempted many owners to convert to alloy wheels. Some owners feel that Rostyle wheels do not look the part, especially as the rust appears, and also swap to alloy wheels. Spridgets do not take too kindly to the fitting of very wide or grippy tyres. The square rear wheel arch versions preclude this anyway; otherwise, the vehicle weight and the original suspension system do not allow for a large increase of grip, or comfort, in all public-road conditions.

Electrics

Many early versions have lost the dynamo, which has been replaced by an alternator along with a change to negative earth. If refurbished properly, there is nothing wrong with the early system, being both reliable and adequate in service. All too often, an update has appeared an easier option for some owners. An upgrade of headlights is popular for well-used Spridgets, if originality is not an issue.

Prior to October 1962, the dynamo drove the rev-counter cable via a small gearbox at the rear. A much sought-after item today if missing.

With a dynamo, a voltage-control box is fitted to regulate the current produced to the battery. This is normally reliable but can fail with age. Below this, the early type fuse box with just two fused circuits.

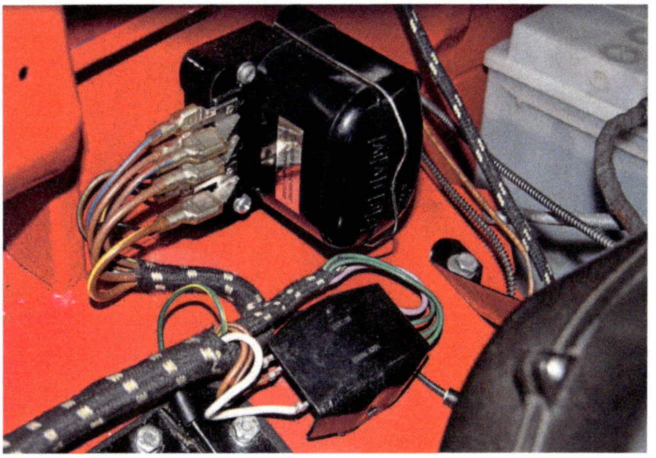

Spares and Services

Spridget owners are very well catered for when it comes to the supply of spare parts. Almost everything from a badge to a body shell is available. The popularity of these cars has not gone unnoticed by the spares industry. From the time when the original manufacturer's stock of spares became exhausted, new suppliers retooled to remanufacture parts. Not everything is available, and some items are still labelled as 'gold dust' or 'hen's teeth', but, essentially, a part can be sourced to keep a Spridget roadworthy if not entirely original. If originality is key, then finding original specification items may be the province of auto jumbles or specialist hoarders. Most of the new parts manufactured today are not from the original manufacturer or to original specification, appearance or materials. Hence, a degree of compromise may be required when restoring or repairing a Spridget. Equally, the quality of current parts is not necessarily the same as an original: some may be better, some not so. The experience of owners' club members has much to say on this subject, some of which is unprintable!

Alternators replaced dynamos from around 1972 on the home market. With the simple electrical demands of a standard-specification Spridget, the earlier dynamo is perfectly adequate, provided it is in good condition.

As well as a plethora of spares suppliers, there are many specialists offering services to owners, including everything from an oil change to a complete restoration. Always check out the reputation of any company that you may seek for professional work. Do not just accept what they say they can do; ask someone who has experience of this. Undoubtedly, the Spridget is one of the best catered for when it comes to spares and services for classic vehicle owners, just so long as you do your homework first.

Tracing the History

Most owners like to know the history of their car. Some may come from the previous owner, along with any accompanying documentation. The original build specification, identification numbers, colour, build dates, destination and options can be obtained from the British Motor Industry Heritage Trust at the Motor Centre, Gaydon, Warwickshire. The DVLA at Swansea may be able to provide copies of previous registration documents from their records. DVLA form V888 can be downloaded from their website. An owners' club may have some information on their car register or valuation service from a previous owner. Some original registration authorities have archived their files; this depends on where the car was originally registered as to whether information is available. The last two letters of the registration identify where the car was originally registered in the UK.

Insurance

In the UK, most owners can take advantage of Agreed Value Classic Car insurance policies. These policies can offer very good and inexpensive cover, providing certain criteria can be met. This may involve having your car valued by your owners' club. There may be annual mileage restrictions and stipulated storage conditions.

Running Costs

Depending on actual build date, vehicles in the UK are exempted from Vehicle Excise Duty, or road tax, if registered as a Historic Vehicle. This now applies to a growing number of Spridgets. Also, vehicles built prior to 1960 no longer require an annual MOT examination. This is a rather a controversial point, but does relieve some owners the cost of having their pre-1960 Sprite examined. Proof of date of build can be obtained from a Heritage Certificate. Fuel consumption should never be an issue, as all the A-Series engines, in standard specification, can offer over 40 mpg under favourable driving conditions. The 1493cc engine has more weight to handle and will therefore use a little more fuel. Depreciation of capital will only be of concern if restoration or purchase costs have exceeded the current value for the particular version. Generally, Spridgets are appreciating in value, some versions much more so than others; but bear in mind the current rate of inflation when looking at this.

Rules & Regulations

These have changed over the years and continue to change in regard to the law and vehicle usage and owner responsibilities. This can make life difficult for the owners of older vehicles to whom these changes are not necessarily directed. Fortunately, owners in the UK have the Federation of British Historic Vehicle Clubs to monitor and campaign on their behalf. Any new proposals and how these may affect older car ownership are fully monitored and considered. The FBHVC consult with the regulators and DVLA to ensure that the continued use of older vehicles is not unduly compromised by any new regulations. As such, ownership and usage of older vehicles in the UK have no specific regulatory restrictions that have not currently been addressed.

Owners' Clubs

Most owners will be members of an appropriate owners' club. However, a potential new owner should also seek the help and guidance that membership can offer. The membership fee is well worth the risk against making an ill-informed purchase of a Spridget. In the UK, the MG Owners Club, the MG Car Club and the Austin-Healey Club are well established clubs that cater for the Marques as a whole. The Midget and Sprite Club is the only

Membership of a club is very useful for advice, as is a mobile phone if you need some unplanned help.

UK-based club that caters exclusively for these cars. Formed in 1983, when Spridgets were pretty much at their lowest ebb, a huge amount of experience, knowledge and support is available for members to take advantage of today. Many other clubs around the world offer help and support also, and an online search will reveal the options for potential members.

Enjoying

There is no shortage of events to attend or places to go to enjoy your car. Joining an appropriate club is essential to get the best from your car; whether to buy, restore, improve or simply enjoy, the clubs are there to support you and your car. You can meet fellow owners, who are never short of good advice and enthusiasm to pass on. It is always nice to receive friendly waves and comments from the public wherever you go, the usual opener being, 'I used to own one of these' and the bottom line being, 'How I miss it'. But you will not be making that mistake, of course!

You need never be alone as a member of a club, though the cost of a round could be expensive!

Conclusions

The British Motor Industry filled a worldwide niche in the small sports-car market. From 1958 to 1979, the Sprite and Midget were major players in this. Ironically, the gap that existed prior to 1958 was restored when both the Midget 1500 and Triumph Spitfire ceased production in 1979 and 1981 respectively.

Despite the high mortality rate of Spridgets, there are survivors. Times and owners may have changed, yet the original objective remains: these are still cars to have fun with on a limited budget.

Today, they are not a throw-away commodity, and owners are more respectful, more caring, perhaps rather older – but still fun-loving. Despite today's driving conditions, there are still plenty of opportunities to enjoy these cars and, indeed, even some new ones. The classic car and the owners' club scene has emerged; these offer owners a whole new world of events to attend, people to meet and friends to make. A new support industry can supply a growing number of parts and services to make ownership an easy proposition. From a badge to a complete body unit, it may prove easier to list what is not available today.

Owners clubs provide a vital and enthusiastic support to owners' needs. The popularity of these cars has brought owners together to form clubs to support whatever owners may need to help purchase, restore, modify and enjoy their cars. Rather mistakenly, some new owners only join a club once they have purchased their Spridget. Anyone at all serious about becoming an owner should join a club before beginning their search.

The big question is, 'Can it be both a fun yet practicable proposition to own one today?' The answer is a most definite, 'yes'. Providing you have considered all the aspects and applied these to your own personal circumstances, then ownership today is something to be enjoyed. Almost certainly, using any of these cars today will not be quite the same as when they were current, and daily commuting, being left out in the open or neglected, or skimped maintenance will not be on the agenda. Likewise, the driving style of, perhaps, a more mature owner of today will ensure that visits into a ditch or through a hedge will also be off the agenda. Owners can still enjoy all the best attributes for which Spridgets became famous. Whether in totally original condition or sensibly modified, Spridgets can survive in most modern driving conditions when the need may arise.

A number of specialist companies offer a growing range of products and services to ensure that Spridgets can not only be enjoyed on the road today and be restored from an impossible state of decay, but that sensible and thoughtfully applied modifications can add to the fun factor. The Spridgets that do survive, or have yet to be restored, are assured of a much safer future in the hands of their enthusiastic owners.

Conceived as a 'fun for the money' small sports car in the middle of the twentieth century, it not only fulfilled that title, but continues to do so well into the twenty-first century.

Is this really the end?